ASTROLOGICAL VOIDS

JANIS HUNTLEY is the author of the best-selling *The Elements of Astrology*. She has been a practising astrologer for over twenty years and gives private readings and classes as well as lecturing in astrology generally.

Astrological Voids

EXPLORING THE MISSING COMPONENTS IN THE BIRTH CHART

JANIS HUNTLEY

Shaftesbury, Dorset • Rockport, Massachusetts

© Janis Huntley 1991

Published in Great Britain in 1991 by
Element Books Limited
Longmead, Shaftesbury, Dorset

Published in the USA in 1991 by
Element Inc
42 Broadway, Rockport, MA 01966

Designed by Roger Lightfoot
Cover design by Max Fairbrother
Phototypeset by Intype, London
Printed and bound in Great Britain by
Billings Ltd, Hylton Road, Worcester

British Library Cataloguing in Publication Data

Huntley, Janis
Astrological voids : exploring the missing
components in the birth chart.
I. Title
133.5

ISBN 1–85230–227–5

Contents

Introduction

The study of astrological voids has been for me a fascinating and extremely enlightening phase of development in my astrological career. The biggest void of all, however, appears to be the lack of reading matter in this area – a fact I discovered in the year 1978, when my son was born with an unaspected Moon. My interest alerted to this hitherto ignored astrological phenomenon, I avidly began to scour the bookshops for information – but to no avail. The few rudimentary phrases I did find concerning unaspected planets were negatively biased and therefore disappointing.

During the next few years I observed the effects of unaspected planets in many birth charts – but in particular those of my son's unaspected Moon. I came to the conclusion that these planets operated very significantly and sometimes – as was the case with my son – tended to dominate a chart, often in a positive rather than negative manner.

With great fascination I began to study all the previously designated 'empty and therefore unimportant' areas of a birth chart, and found that much information concerning a subject's basic characteristics, attitudes and inherent needs in life, as well as karmic obligations, could be gleaned from such study. As a result, the whole – rather than part – of a birth chart becomes alive. Nothing is irrelevant, nothing is disregarded. On a physical level, if a human being is born without an arm or a leg, this lack will inevitably affect him greatly throughout life – it cannot be ignored. Voids within a birth chart should therefore never be overlooked. We all possess certain voids within our birth charts – without them we are not complete. I hope, therefore, that as you read through this book, you will discover new facets of your present and previous lives, which will open up many new vistas within your development.

1

Unoccupied Houses

The houses of a birth chart represent the many-faceted areas of human life. Some modern-day astrologers prefer to omit the usage of a regular house system in favour of an interpretation based purely upon the 'planets in sign and aspect' combinations but in my opinion astrology without house division gives a bleak, over-technical delineation of a birth chart. Significantly more information concerning a person's lifestyle can be gleaned by studying the houses – both tenanted and untenanted – than by using the planet and sign alone. I consider the tradition of house division to be of supreme importance in any birth chart interpretation. For many years now, I have practised the Equal House system of division. It has the advantages of simplicity, regularity and aesthetic appeal, but virtually all methods of house division have their own commendable qualities, and I firmly believe that any system is better than none at all.

At the time of writing, there are ten planetary bodies used in the erection of a birth chart (Sun, Moon, Mercury, Venus, Mars, Jupiter, Saturn, Uranus, Neptune and Pluto). Some astrologers calculate the position of the planetoid Chiron, but due to conflicting opinion as to its sign rulership, and the fact that it is not a true star, planet or moon, I tend to omit it from the chart.

It is an extremely rare occurrence to find all ten planets posited in ten separate houses. Most people possess at least three empty houses, the majority four or five, and some as many as seven or eight – the latter usually applying to those subjects whose chart shape can be categorized as a 'Bundle'. It can be very disappointing for a person with such a shaping or many empty houses who, upon approaching an astrologer for a reading, discovers that many important areas of his life are supposedly meaningless! Astrologers who only interpret the positions of the planets are losing out on much valuable information depicted by the unoccupied houses.

GUIDELINES

It must always be borne in mind that, in common with most other areas of astrological interpretation, unoccupied houses can be analysed on several levels. The two accentuated in this book are the physical/mundane plane and the spiritual/karmic plane. Both are highly relevant and interconnected with each other.

A high proportion of empty houses (seven or more) within a birth chart indicates intensity, single-mindedness, dedication, obsessiveness, habitual responses, lack of adaptability, and powerful ambition, even when other factors in the chart may suggest differently. A low proportion of empty houses indicates versatility, changeability, possible lack of concentration, diversity of interests and talents, complexity, and broadness of view.

On a karmic level, each house represents an area of life in which the subject may, or may not, need to be tested during any given lifetime. Houses occupied by planets suggest a strong karmic testing ground, whereas unoccupied houses appear to represent those areas of life which have passed the testing stage during a previous lifetime, or which at least are not a high priority in this one.

MUNDANE CLASSIFICATION

Unoccupied houses are not boring, uninteresting or lacking in purpose – especially as far as the subject is concerned. Clients do express explicit needs over monetary concerns when they have no planets in the second or the eighth, and they do possess opinions on relationship matters when they possess no planets in the seventh or fifth – but, on a very general level, as listed below, the unoccupied houses of a birth chart usually depict those areas of life which the subject accepts with equanimity or does not need to express to any great extent.

Unoccupied first: Uncluttered personality true to sign on cusp. In harmony with outer appearance and projection of self-image.

Unoccupied second: Money, possessions and values are not vital to the subject. Financial circumstances either completely assured or totally irrelevant.

Unoccupied third: No essential desire to communicate or travel on a daily, mundane level. Relatives and siblings easily accepted or not integrated into subject's lifestyle.

Unoccupied fourth: Often prefers to be away from the home environment. Actual home setting not important. One of the parents, usually father, not too significant in life.

Unoccupied fifth: No innate urge to procreate. Romantic, sporting and creative instincts either take a back seat or are transmuted into other areas of life.

Unoccupied sixth: Definitely not a workaholic! Rarely worries unduly about health or work matters, and often possesses strong constitution.

Unoccupied seventh: Able to live life equally well in either a married or single state. This person enjoys independence and is less likely to 'hang on' to outworn relationships.

Unoccupied eighth: Not dependent upon others' emotions or financial resources for their own well-being. Unlikely to become involved in extremely intense, obsessive or over-emotional relationships.

Unoccupied ninth: Higher learning, expansive philosophies and extensive travelling are areas of life which this person accepts readily enough but will not be driven to experience on a personal level.

Unoccupied tenth: Represents a person who does not strive to assert himself ambitiously or need to be admired as a status symbol. Detachment and/or acceptance towards mother-figure.

Unoccupied eleventh: Equally at ease when possessing many friends or none at all, but unlikely to encourage close liaisons or to become entrenched in group situations.

Unoccupied twelfth: Lesser evolved souls usually find planets posited here rather difficult to handle. Voids, however, tend to add balance and strength on both a mental and physical plane.

RELATED HOUSES

When analysing an empty house, a deeper interpretation can be achieved by studying certain houses in conjunction with others. Houses in opposition to one another possess many similar areas of expression; for instance, both the second and the eighth houses relate to differing aspects of emotions, finances and possessions, whilst the sixth and the twelfth can both signify health concerns – the sixth in a direct manner – the twelfth indirectly through hospital or institutional connections. If both are empty, the representative qualities are very minor or unimportant constituents of the subject's innate characteristics. If, however, one is empty and the other occupied by one or more planets, then an imbalance exists and the subject can become overconcerned or obsessed by the areas of life represented by the occupied house and completely neglect or fail to recognize the qualities of the empty house.

The second, sixth and tenth houses should be studied in unison when endeavouring to interpret the subject's working status. The uncommon (but not rare by any means) combination of all three houses unoccupied denotes a total lack of interest in working, financial and status-orientated situations, but it does not necessarily indicate a lack of ability within these areas. Most men need to work in order to earn money, and those with this configuration will do so, despite the lack of planets in these houses. When the second is unoccupied with both the sixth and tenth occupied, the subject is ambitious and mindful of working needs, but unconcerned with the financial rewards of his efforts. The tenth house occupied with both the second and sixth empty signifies an extremely ambitious and assertive person to whom status and success are more important factors than job satisfaction and monetary gains. If, however, the second house only is occupied, then it is financial security which is the vital factor, and the subject is capable of working hard and asserting himself in a career in order to satisfy his strong monetary requirements.

Likewise, the third, seventh and eleventh houses should be looked at simultaneously. All of them are pertinent to communication within relationships at some level – the third denoting siblings, distant relatives and neighbours, the seventh marital and business partners and the eleventh friends and close associates. A chart possessing voids in all three areas relates to an individual who seemingly has no desire to form relationships on a communicative level, but the presence of a strong (occupied) eighth or fifth house would signify the subject's mode of forming close liaisons would be through emotional and/or physical contact. A subject with several planets in the eleventh and none in the seventh may find it easier to communicate mentally with casual associates than close partners. The third house occupied, with voids in both the eleventh and seventh could indicate that attachments to relatives takes precedence over all other relationships.

The fourth, eighth and twelfth houses also project similar attitudes. These are secretive or closed-in houses, indicative of strong, but repressed emotions and deep intuitive reactions. A total void in these areas tends to render the subject more open and creative in his expressions and less liable to emotional instability, but lacking in depth of feeling, unless the chart is well represented by water signs. An occupied eighth with no fourth or twelfth suggests a person who chooses to express his emotional needs purely through sexual activity, whereas an occupied fourth with empty twelfth and eighth houses seeks his emotional security from within the confines of his own home and the boundaries of his upbringing. When the twelfth house is occupied and the fourth and eighth empty, the subject can become reclusive on an emotional level, with a tendency to live in a secret world of fantasy and imagination. His feelings are deep, but difficult to demonstrate.

The first, fifth and ninth houses are all areas of assertive self-expression, the first through the realms of appearance and personality, the fifth through creative endeavours and the ninth through expansive, mental transference. Planets in the first with no fifth or ninth indicate an individual who can be obsessively concerned with his own personal effect upon the outside world. As a result vanity or self-centredness can manifest. The compulsively creative lifestyle of a strong fifth house individual with no first or ninth to help generate a balance can become dangerous – over-large families, too much risk-taking and fatalistic love affairs are but three of the many possible conditions applicable to this combination. Too much ninth with no fifth or first can manifest in over-zealous religious or philosophical attitudes which are difficult to integrate into the outer expression of personality and into creative endeavours. Much travelling and/or learning may be undertaken with very little personal or creative accomplishment.

Another combination well worth noting is that of the fifth, seventh and eighth houses. All three have some bearing on close, emotional and marital relationships. A lack of planets in all three houses usually implies a certain detachment or disinterest in forming close relationships. Sometimes it is the general physical and mental circumstances of the subject which seem to deny emotional contacts. This phenomenon was unexpectedly revealed to me about eight years ago when I gave a series of astrological talks to various societies for the physically and mentally handicapped. The audiences were warm and enthusiastic and even the mentally handicapped seemed to grasp the essence of drawing up a birth chart remarkably well, but virtually all of the examples I analysed at random on the board were devoid of fifth, seventh and eighth house planetary connections. The discovery was no coincidence – it made much sense, because a very high percentage of these people were unable, due to their handicaps, to form normal emotional and physical unions.

When only one of these houses is occupied it signifies quite emphatically the area in which the subject chooses to connect on a relationship level. This is probably the area in which they have struggled during a past existence and are in need of further testing. Fifth house only suggests over-romantic instincts and a tendency for casual affairs or marital infidelity, whereas seventh house only indicates a person who revels in the permanency and closeness of a binding commitment. The eighth house subject with no fifth or seventh tends to view relationships on a deeply emotional and physical level, but has a tendency to become obsessed by the sexual aspects of the relationship.

The fourth and tenth houses, in addition to being opposites, must also be assimilated as a partnership when assessing the parental influence upon an individual. When one of these houses is empty and the other occupied, as so often occurs, it indicates that one parent played a more prominent role in the child's upbringing than the other – the empty house signifying the parent who was absent, detached or disinclined to demonstrate much parental love or authority.

The combinations are many and they should all be studied in conjunction with each other.

HOUSE CUSP RULERS

When studying both occupied and unoccupied houses, it is vital that the ruler of the sign on the cusp of the relevant house is located and taken into account. Cusp rulers are always important, and ancient astrologers based much of their interpretation upon these positions. When dealing with unoccupied houses, however, their relevance can become crucial, especially when the ruler of the sign on the cusp of the house is prominent in the chart (angular, highly aspected, unaspected and so on). The house in which the cusp ruler is placed is usually the area of life which succeeds in conveying the qualities of the empty house. For example an unoccupied seventh house, with the cusp ruler posited in the fifth, could indicate that the subject regarded romance, creativity and lovemaking as vitally important to the success of a permanent relationship. Children, too, would inevitably play an essential role when assessing the potential for an enduring relationship.

The position of the house cusp ruler can be so important that it may even dominate a chart. Many a time, after having been asked to guess a person's Ascendant, I discover I have selected the sign in which the ruler of the Ascendant is placed. When the sign containing the Ascendant is empty, or there is no angular twelfth house planet, the subject's outer personality is likely to embody a high proportion of the qualities of the sign in which the ruler is placed.

When there are no planets in the fourth or tenth, the position of the cusp ruler is often indicative of the relevant parent. (I consider the fourth to relate to the father and the tenth the mother, but the roles can easily be reversed, and no rigid rule should be applied.) It is very unusual not to be able to ascertain the Sun sign or the Ascendant of a parent after having looked at the sign on the cusp of the 4th/IC (or 10th/MC), any planets placed therein, and the position of the house cusp ruler. Sometimes a parent will be strongly indicated by two or even all three of these factors. If no connection can be found it is worth looking at the positions of the Sun and Moon, which can represent the father and mother respectively, although I find them somewhat unreliable sources of information when used on their own.

The ancient system of determining the character and sex of offspring through studying the fifth house in relation to the first child, the seventh in relation to the second, the ninth to the third, and so on, does seem to possess some validity as regards the character of the child, but not the sex. When using the Equal house system all the signs on the cusps of the alternate houses, as used, will be either positive or negative. The method of relating a positive sign to a male child and a negative sign to a female child is therefore extremely unreliable as very few families bear children which are exclusively of one sex.

I have found this system works much better when the ruler of the sign on the cusp of the relevant house is used, especially when the house is unoccupied. After studying quite a few families with three or more children I discerned that by using the ruler of the house cusp in conjunction with the sign and any planets posited therein, the children's Ascendants or Sun signs were nearly always apparent within the mother's chart – and often within the father's chart too – though men's charts generally tend to be less reliable in this respect.

My own family of four children provides a 100 per cent authentication of this theory in action. My fifth house cusp is Aquarius and my eldest child is an Aquarian. The planet Mars placed in this sign also has much bearing upon her character. My seventh house, with Aries on the cusp, is empty. The ruler, Mars, is placed in Aquarius, as mentioned, and my second child is also a Sun Aquarian with several Mars qualities (Mars in

Aries, Scorpio rising). My third child's character is represented by all three factors relating to my ninth house
– Gemini the sign on the cusp, Mercury the house cusp
ruler, and Uranus the planet placed therein. He is a Sun
Piscean and Mercury the ruler of my ninth is placed in
Pisces. He indirectly exhibits many Geminian qualities
by possessing a stellium (three planets) in the third house
(the natural house of Gemini), a Splash type shaping
which is indicative of a Mercurial character, and the
planet Jupiter placed in Gemini. Uranus is placed exactly
on his Midheaven. The sign of Leo, on the cusp of my
eleventh house with Saturn and Pluto placed therein,
very strongly represents my fourth child, born with four
planets including the Sun in Leo. Saturn is angular
within her chart and Pluto forms a powerful conjunction
to the Moon. The ruler of my eleventh is the Sun, which
is placed in Pisces, and this daughter possesses a strong,
angular Neptune.

This high level of connections is not apparent in every
family but the use of the house cusp rulers certainly adds
a further dimension to the analysis of offspring potential.

RULERSHIP INTERPRETATION

The following delineations apply purely to the house and
the position of the house cusp ruler. They do not take
into account the nature of the planetary ruler or the
qualities of the signs in which the planets are placed, or
the signs on the cusps of the empty houses. When pro-
ducing a complete interpretation it should be remembered that the signs of the zodiac basically represent
avenues of expression through which the energies of the
planets can operate. For example Gemini needs to
express through verbal or written communication,
whereas Cancer needs to express through the feelings
and emotions. These modes of expression through the
signs, plus the natural energy of the planet, should be
analysed in conjunction with the influence of the cusp
rulers and their placements. Although the interpretations

are considered to be applicable to unoccupied houses, they may also be very appropriate when the house in question is occupied.

THE FIRST HOUSE

The ruler of the first house cusp (Ascendant) is usually the most significant of the rulership placements. It is very common for this planet to dominate a chart even when there are planets posited in the first house. This is the area which rules our outer demeanour and appearance or, in more general terms, our 'personality' and it is as such a crucial factor in human psychological development.

The position of the ruler of the first house is usually the area in which a subject is more easily able to project his or her own personality. It is an unfortunate fact, however, that most people tend to judge a book by its cover or another human being by the image they project. An individual will be happier and more fulfilled, therefore, if when possessing a normally likeable, sunny Ascendant such as Leo, the ruler is placed in a complementary sign and house (Sun in Sagittarius in the fifth, for instance). On the other hand, if the Sun is placed in Capricorn in the sixth house, with many adverse aspects, this subject will inevitably feel uncomfortable within himself and have more difficulty in expressing the outgoing Leo nature.

In order for the fundamental principle of rulership interpretation to be more easily understood, it is useful to think of the ruler of the house in question being 'taken' to the house it occupies, where it sets up residence and is allowed an outlet for its expression. This theory also helps the astrologer to differentiate between the subtle differences in interpretation of parallel configurations – for instance, the ruler of the first house being placed in the second, as compared to the ruler of the second being placed in the first. In the first instance the personality is taken to the second house and utilized within financial affairs, but in the second instance the financial interests are conveyed to the area representing the personality and subsequently these prerequisites are incorporated within the subject's self-image. The first instance would tend to 'quieten' the personality and render the subject more unobtrusive on an outer level, whereas the second instance would enliven the personality, especially where financial affairs were concerned.

Ruler of the Empty First

Placed in the second: The personality is more easily projected when monetary or financial affairs are in debate. Possessions, money and earning capacity are important to the subject's self-image and he may be able to earn money through the expression of his personality. This position should add a certain amount of stability, stoicism, passivity and introspection to the personality.

Placed in the third: The subject enjoys communicating and sharing his thoughts on a very open level with relatives and neighbours. The personality and appearance become more pronounced when the subject is indulging in stimulating conversation, especially when it is centred around himself. Daily travel and education are important outlets in which the individual feels able to expand his personality.

Placed in the fourth: The personality is toned down and rendered more sensitive and quiet with the subject only truly becoming himself when ensconced within his own home environment. Much depends upon the planets and signs involved, but it is possible for a duality of personality to arise – the individual being quiet on the surface but dominant or tyrannical in the home. The subject's personality will be firmly engraved in the home structure, which may seem empty without his presence.

Placed in the fifth: This house very much complements the first, so regardless of which planet is involved, the subject will to some extent project a balanced, sociable personality. This person thoroughly enjoys immersing himself in fifth house pursuits – creativity, lovemaking, children, sporting interests. The personal planets and Jupiter tend to project a more carefree image, but any ruling planet placed here produces a strong personality. The subject may, however, be prone to childish or immature behaviour, and could be reckless in his pursuit of love.

Placed in the sixth: This produces a much more serious and relatively quiet personality, although the subject is capable of projecting himself very well when involved in a working environment or when offering himself for service in some manner. This person is usually a hard worker (a possible exception to this occurring when Venus is the ruler of the first) who is also aware of the need to remain healthy. Animals respond kindly to this individual.

Placed in the seventh: Although the personality is brightened and rendered more communicative with this position, the subject is always in danger of allowing his own personality to become swallowed up by his partner's. The individual's initiative, enterprise and individuality can be lost as the partner's mode of self-expression gradually becomes his own. This person needs relationships as much as a duck needs water, but once involved they run the risk of being 'drowned' by their partner's wishes. It is very important for these individuals to learn how to integrate the energy of the relevant planet into their own constitution.

Placed in the eighth: The sensitivity and emotional outlook of the personality is deepened. In his quiet way, the subject may endeavour to analyse his own personality in order to understand his strong, but usually unmentioned desires in life. This placement adds calmness and astuteness to the outer demeanour, though there may be a seething mass of emotions lurking beneath the surface. His seemingly thoughtful responses can make others inclined to be generous towards him.

Placed in the ninth: This placement can help the personality to be expressed on a highly expansive level. It adds confidence and intellect to any Ascendant. Travel and learning are undertaken with zest and enthusiasm and a certain amount of impatience. The subject expresses himself well when undertaking philosophical, educational or religious pursuits. If fire or air signs dominate the chart the subject is in danger of being labelled eccentric.

Placed in the tenth: A powerful desire for recognition is indicated by this placement. The subject is capable of using his personality in order to achieve his aims and ambitions. Depending upon the planet and sign placement, this person may be well-loved, feared or extremely disliked, but nobody will be totally immune to his commanding presence. In his overriding longing to succeed the subject must be careful that he does not deplete his personality to such an extent that he has very little to express about other areas of life.

Placed in the eleventh: This subject employs his personality in the ardent pursuit of friendships and group activities. This will be done speedily and impatiently if Mars is the ruler of the first, slowly and cautiously if the ruler is Saturn. But whatever planet is involved, the culmination of his effort is much the same – an ingratiation into the lives and activities of friends and groups. Depending on the planet and the method used as indicated by the sign on the Ascendant, he may be very well liked or much disliked, but in either case his skills will often be regarded by the group as indispensable.

Placed in the twelfth: It can be very obstructive for a person to be born with the ruler of the open, self-assertive first house placed within the quiet seclusion of the twelfth. The restraints felt by the subject when endeavouring to express his personality can be enormous. Unless the planet is within 8 degrees of the Ascendant (angular), the subject may be regarded as quiet, aloof, difficult to understand or to reach on an emotional level. This is especially the case when one of the five personal planets (Sun, Moon, Mercury, Venus or Mars) is the ruler of the first house. It does not always manifest in limitation, however. Very often the subject enjoys his own company, and the personality can be expressed through twelfth house activities such as charities, healing, hospitals, prisons and large, enclosed organizations.

THE SECOND HOUSE

Everybody possesses an attitude or opinion about the financial/material resources of life. To many individuals money is the source of power, success and happiness, whereas to others it represents the root of all evil. Generally speaking an individual with an empty second house is not overly concerned with financial security except in the area in which the ruler is placed. All the basic needs, values and intrinsic desires for money and possessions are usually channelled into this one area. Indirectly, therefore, money can be of great significance to a subject with an empty second house.

Ruler of Empty Second

Placed in the first: The subject exhibits his need for financial security within his personality. He may consider that his self-image is enhanced by openly communicating upon financial matters, earning capacity, accumulation of possessions and so on. His security is based on the fact that he is seen to be financially secure and stable, whereas in truth, he cares very little for the material assets of life.

Placed in the third: Finances become important to this individual within all third house matters. Relatives, siblings and neighbours can all benefit (or suffer, if the planet concerned makes challenging aspects) at the hands of the individual. He may be more concerned about the material quality of other people's lives than his own, and be of help in their financial progression in life. He may enjoy spending money on education, daily travel, car maintenance and mundane activities – all of which are important issues in his life.

Placed in the fourth: The subject's innate need and desire for money, possessions and security is lifted into the home situation, where much may be spent (or saved if Saturn is the ruler). This person is likely to accumulate a mass of possessions within the home, but may be totally unconcerned about the quality of the clothes he wears, or the acquisition of other luxuries in life, but what he does acquire he hangs on to relentlessly. He may become vulnerable, over-emotional or obsessive about his needs. Money or possessions may readily be given to a parent. This is an unobtrusive but extremely shrewd placement.

Placed in the fifth: As with the ruler of the second in the first this is a confident, outgoing placement. The subject tends to spend most of his money on fifth house concerns such as children, hobbies, creative outlets and romantic attachments. There could be a risk of feckless gambling with this position, because the subject cares little about his own financial security. Money is considered well spent on anything which enhances his social outlets in life, and he can be generous to a fault, if Moon, Venus, Mars or Jupiter is the ruler of the second. In other areas of life, however, he could react in a totally reverse manner.

Placed in the sixth: This person enjoys working and is usually willing to plough his money into schemes or projects that he considers worthwhile. To him the satisfaction of a job well done is far more important than the financial rewards. Money or possessions also become relevant where his health is concerned. Private medical care, alternative health treatment, exercise equipment and so on, are of great importance in his life. The subject may give quite willingly to co-workers, animals and health organizations, but be stringent where other matters are concerned.

Placed in the seventh: Anything that the subject earns or owns is regarded as belonging to his partner. One of his main mottoes in life may be 'share and share alike'. Joint bank accounts, shared business outlets and combined ownership means security to this individual, who is willing to give all to his partner if necessary. The partner, however, must be prepared to take all, including the subject's values and opinions. Another phrase likely to be often on the lips of this subject is 'My partner and I believe that . . .'

Placed in the eighth: This rulership position is similar to the seventh house placement – shared money, possessions and business concerns, for instance, but there is much more giving on the part of the subject to the eighth house individual (this can be the partner, or any person with whom the subject is involved in a close physical or emotional relationship). The subject enjoys spending or giving out either possessions or emotional responses to the other person, who is quite capable of taking all and giving very little in return. The persistence and devotion which these subjects are capable of rendering does, however, eventually bring them their own financial rewards. Money may also be spent on deep studies, occult and psychological pursuits, underground activities, births and funerals.

Placed in the ninth: The subject enjoys holidays, travelling and learning and feels the need to spend money on these activities. Books concerning these subjects are considered vital, as are curios, antiques and items produced and bought in foreign lands. A desire to give money or possessions to foreign people, especially those in need, may be apparent, as could be a need to relate to a specific religious denomination in which they can offer their values, services and financial support.

Placed in the tenth: Money, possessions and values are

brought into the area of career. This subject enjoys owning and financing his own business and will spend great amounts in order to further his own aims and ambitions. Money and luxury commodities may be seen as status symbols. This position, more than any other placement of the ruler of the second, gives an impression of great financial needs and interests, when in reality the subject cares little for financial security but yearns to see his name emblazoned in lights. As with the ruler of the second in the fourth, this placement indicates an above-average expenditure on one of the parents.

Placed in the eleventh: The subject feels obliged to spend money on friends, and/or give financial support to organizations. He may find himself continually pushed into responsible group positions, such as that of treasurer. To this person the motto 'a friend in need is a friend indeed' is highly applicable. He is always willing to help, but will also try to impress his own values and opinions on the members of his group.

Placed in the twelfth: Financial security does not come easily with this placement. The subject often feels a strong urge to sacrifice his own material needs for the sake of others. Money and possessions are easily discarded or given to charities. In some cases the subject may not feel worthy enough to be a wealthy, secure person. This is a perfect placement for the donation of blood and human organs and for the expenditure of money on hospital or institutional fees. Less evolved subjects, however, may use money for underhand purposes and be capable of financially orientated criminal acts. The subject may also be very secretive about his financial situation and earning powers.

THIRD HOUSE

An empty third house is usually indicative of an individual who does not concern himself too much with communication. He accepts and takes for granted the areas of life represented by the this house, and although he may not be gifted in this area, there are rarely communication problems. Relatives, siblings and neighbours are readily accepted, or casually ignored. The subject does not feel an inner need to co-operate, or burden himself with the requirements of these people. Education is readily assimilated, but often in a detached or offhand manner. Similarly, any form of short-distance or mundane travelling is regarded an unimportant. If the need arises the subject is able to show willing, but otherwise he will not concern himself. If the first, seventh and eleventh are also empty, the subject may be extremely uncommunicative on a verbal or written level.

Ruler of Empty Third

Placed in the first: The subject may force himself to communicate on a light level in order that his self-image is projected favourably. He may talk animatedly about relatives, pastimes and daily events which in reality interest him very little. This person cares greatly about his personality structure and is able to utilize all third house matters to his own advantage in this respect. As a result he may seem more altruistic than he truly is. Providing, however, that his relatives can relate to his often 'gushing' personality, he will take them under his wing, and treat them in the same vein as himself.

Placed in the second: All third house matters become a source of financial or possessive interest. Money can be earned indirectly through relatives, siblings or neighbours, or through writing, teaching or communication. The belongings and values of relatives may become pertinent to the individual's own lifestyle. He may be willing to travel, or learn, for the sake of relatives or siblings, but usually it is the subject who benefits financially from anything that he may do for these people.

Placed in the fourth: Relatives, siblings and neighbours feature prominently in the subject's home-life. An aunt,

uncle or grandparent may be wholly or partially responsible for the individual's upbringing. Education and
learning may be better absorbed when undertaken within
the home environment, where the subject feels safe and
more able to communicate and express himself verbally.
Unless it benefits his home environment, daily travel will
be embarked upon reluctantly.

Placed in the fifth: The subject enjoys social interchanges
with his relatives and neighbours. He may try to per-
suade them to 'join in' his activities, whether they be
mental, physical or sporting. There are strong possibilit-
ies of romantic attachments occurring between the subject and a relative or neighbour. Short journeys and pleasure trips will be readily undertaken by the subject when
he is accompanied by a sibling, relative or neighbour.
Learning and education become easier and more fun
when the individual is socially stimulated.

Placed in the sixth: Third house matters are activated by
the sixth house work situations and health interests. The
subject is keen to introduce his neighbours and relatives
to his work environment and possibly work in close
conjunction with these contacts, thereby improving his
relationships with them. Short journeys and daily routine
communications which are normally regarded as trivial
or unnecessary, are undertaken with zest when related
to work requirements. Relatives and neighbours are
likely to be concerned about any health problems which
the subject may develop, and to show a keen interest in
any pets that he might own.

Placed in the seventh: The subject pushes all his communicative tendencies onto his partner. He may be reticent
with his neighbours and relatives but expect his 'other
half' to react responsively towards them. Short-distance
travel and education become enjoyable (or difficult if a
planet such as Saturn is involved) when expressed with
the partner. Both as a child and an adult, this person
depends upon a very close companion to provide the
stimulation and communication that may be lacking

within himself. Permanent, binding relationships with relatives could occur.

Placed in the eighth: Siblings, relatives and neighbours are all put under pressure by the subject's emotional, physical and financial requirements, which can be very demanding. The subject expects and receives help from third house contacts. There may be emotional undercurrents or intense involvements between the individual and his relatives. Communication and short-distance travel will only willingly be undertaken when other people's finances or emotions are concerned. Inheritances from relatives are likely.

Placed in the ninth: This is an expansive, helpful combination which is usually good for communication on a higher level. The subject strongly desires to bring everything mundane out into the open and express himself on a broad, philosophical or religious level. He enjoys making mountains out of molehills and treating a day out in Southend as if it were a visit to the other side of the earth. He enjoys the company of his relatives and neighbours whilst communicating and travelling.

Placed in the tenth: In much the same way as when the ruler of the third is placed in the sixth, the subject enjoys the company of his relatives and friends within his career environment. On a more negative level he may actually exploit them in order to satisfy his own needs and ambitions. Daily travel and education are tolerated within the subject's working life only if he feels that his career will be enhanced by such activities. There may be much contact between the subject's relatives and his mother.

Placed in the eleventh: Relatives and neighbours become embroiled within the social and group activities of the individual, who may be very persuasive in his endeavours to make them take on positions of responsibility within such groups. Because the subject is able to communicate more freely with such contacts, he tends to regard them as his closest friends. Short-distance travel and education are readily pursued for the sake of a sibling, relative or neighbour.

Placed in the twelfth: Open, positive houses such as the third can find expression extremely difficult when the ruler is placed within the confines of the twelfth house. One or more of the subject's siblings or other relatives may suffer from twelfth house problems – imprisonment, hospitalization, secrecy, self-sacrifice or mental illness. Any of these situations may actually be caused, either directly or indirectly by the subject's inadequacies. Short-distance journeys and education are more likely to be experienced in twelfth house places such as hospitals and other institutions, or through twelfth house activities such as secrecy and self-sacrifice. The subject may unwittingly draw his relatives and friends into his own escapist world.

THE FOURTH HOUSE

An empty fourth house usually indicates an individual who is not attached emotionally or physically to the home environment. Be it a caravan or a stately mansion, the actual structure and position of the residence is relatively unimportant as far as the subject is concerned. Wherever the ruler is placed, however, is the area in which the subject feels 'at home' and is likely to be able to relate to a home environment.

This house also represents basic emotions and one of the parents, but a void in this area does not necessarily detract from the emotional sensitivity of the subject, or decree that one of the parents is missing. It does, however, suggest that one of the parents, very often the father, is either readily accepted and loved by the subject, regardless of all faults, or that the parent in question has shunned much of the responsibility of the child's upbringing. (This is purely the subjective viewpoint of the native and may not necessarily represent the 'actual' situation.) Individuals who possess voids in both the fourth and the tenth houses are invariably independent, strong-willed, and strangely relaxed about their relationship (or lack of same) with their parents. They are born survivors who can adapt well to a life which does not include close parental ties or a fixed abode. This apparent detachment often adds a restless, wandering quality to the subject's character.

Ruler of Empty Fourth

Placed in the first: The quiet, home-orientated and emotional responses of the fourth house are brought out into the open for all to see. It is important to the subject's concept of his own self-image that he is seen to be a home-loving, warm and caring person who respects his parents' wishes. This person will strive to achieve a happy home-life and a luxurious residence in order that he may feel 'normal' and readily accepted as a likeable person, but the end result may be a lifestyle that is inwardly distasteful and completely unable to satisfy his true needs.

Placed in the second: The issues of home and parents are brought into the realms of financial awareness. The subject may view his home and parents as means by which he can expand his own earning capacity or financial security. One of the parents, in particular, may be regarded as a possession. The sign on the cusp of the second and the planet placed therein will indicate whether this possessive attitude is demonstrated in a caring or callous manner. The subject may insist (quietly or otherwise) that one of the parents support his materialistic endeavours. It would appear to be the subject who gains most from this contact, but more often than not the parent is a willing partner.

Placed in the third: The subject feels at home with his siblings, relatives and neighbours and may prefer to reside with them. His upbringing probably involved many relatives willing to act as surrogate parents if necessary. The subject is likely to be very restless in any home situation, and may even travel around from home to home, and relative to relative, in a vagrant-like manner. He is highly unlikely to bear his parents any grudges, but he will rarely act demonstratively towards them.

Placed in the fifth: This person feels little attachment or responsibility towards his home environment or father. His motto might be 'home is where the fun is'. Any home that can allow him to be creative, fun-loving, demonstrative and childlike will appeal greatly to him, and he will actively ensure that his own home is suited to these needs. Sports rooms, swimming pools, exercise areas, tennis courts, children's nurseries, are but a few of the commodities he considers desirable in a home. One of the parents is likely to be immature or childlike, but the subject can cope quite well with this anomaly.

Placed in the sixth: Home situations and one of the parents are transported into the area of work and health. The subject feels emotionally secure if he is somehow able to connect the two areas of life. He may endeavour to bring his father into his place of work, or even work in partnership with him. The subject may regard a certain area of his work environment as belonging totally to himself, and even attempt to call it 'home' and decorate the area as if it were a home. Objects and articles from his home will certainly be displayed on his desk or place of work. He will readily discuss home situations when he is safely ensconced in this work environment.

Placed in the seventh: 'Home is where the partner is' should be his person's motto. The individual is willing to live anywhere and under any conditions providing he is emotionally involved in a loving, caring partnership. One of the subject's parents may reside in the same house as the couple and be a source of fulfilment or limitation – depending upon the planet involved and the aspects it makes. The subject, who may be emotionally detached in most areas of life, finds it extremely difficult to achieve this emotional independence within the relationship.

Placed in the eighth: This placement adds to the emotional intensity and introverted qualities which the subject possesses. The usual easy acceptance of home situations and upbringing tends to become more tense when the ruler is placed in this position. Home becomes important when related to the partner's emotional and financial needs. The subject may receive (and expect) help from the father as regards to the partner's financial or emotional problems.

Placed in the ninth: Home needs to be as far away from the country of birth as possible. If not possible, then the subject should at least possess an overseas holiday home of some description. The subject is not truly happy or 'at home' unless he is residing in a foreign land. Some of this restlessness may be transmuted into extensive travelling or expansive learning, but the home abroad is the ultimate realization. The subject's father is often of foreign descent himself and is encouraged to accompany his offspring on distant journeys. Home situations and security requirements are brought out into the open, debated and discussed and often utilized within the subject's expansive learning processes.

Placed in the tenth: The subject views his place of career as his home, and can become over-emotional or ultra-sensitive to criticism in this respect. Any problems arising within his home situation are taken to work where he is able to reflect upon them more easily and sort them out. This placement very often indicates that one parent – usually the father – has taken on the role of both parents in the subject's upbringing, and has been instrumental in encouraging the ambitions and career fulfilment of his offspring.

Placed in the eleventh: Friends and group activities represent a haven of peace, security and 'oneness' to the person with this combination. He feels at ease and more able to express his innermost emotions when situated within the homes of his friends and the environment of group activities. One of the parents may become

involved in the subject's group interests and eventually
maintain a true friendship with his offspring.

Placed in the twelfth: Although the ruler of the fourth is
supposedly at ease when situated in this harmonious
water house, it is often a difficult placement for the
subject and/or his parents – one of whom may be insti-
tutionalized, imprisoned or hospitalized at some critical
juncture of his life or totally absent from his child's
upbringing. Sometimes the subject himself is fated to
spend time in an institution. Home situations and problems are viewed as matters to be kept secret. The subject
may even spend a portion of his life without a true
home, or donate his home to charity.

THE FIFTH HOUSE

In many respects the fifth house seems to pertain to all
that is pleasurable in life – sociable entertainment, fun,
creativity, children, romantic attachments, sport and
gambling. It is the natural house of the Sun and as such
should be regarded as an extremely important area of
the birth chart. Planets situated here indicate a love of
activity. It can, therefore, be somewhat disappointing to
find a lack of planets in this 'vital' house. It must always
be borne in mind, however, that people with a void in
this area do not necessarily consider any of the above
mentioned objectives in life as being of prime importance. They do not usually seek pleasure in the same
generalized, enthusiastic manner as those with planets
posited in this house. As with all other unoccupied
houses, the position of the planet ruling the fifth house
cusp is extremely important, as this is the area in which
the subject will tend to nurture all his sociable and
romantic instincts.

A person with planets in the fifth is naturally romantic,
creative and easily stimulated into physical or mental
activity depending on the planet involved, though these
characteristics may not always be readily apparent or
utilized with ease, as is the case with planets like Saturn

or Pluto. A person with no planets in the fifth, on the other hand, may seem to be immune to fifth house needs or project them into a concentrated area.

It is very rare for a female with an empty fifth house to desire a large family. In the few instances where the subject has more than two children there are usually other mitigating factors involved, such as submission to a partner's overriding need to raise a family. An extremely fertile sign on the cusp of the fifth (Cancer, Scorpio or Pisces) can raise the number of children conceived, especially when the ruler is also placed within a water sign, but the true desire to create and care for children may be lacking.

Ruler of Empty Fifth

Placed in the first: The subject gives the impression that he is a sociable, fun-loving individual with a strong creative urge. Females with this placement usually profess a strong desire to bear children, and males will categorically state how much they enjoy the company of children. In both cases, the subjects' outer manifestation of fifth house activity is very often a delusion which is difficult to break – so convinced are these subjects that their open expression of strong fifth house needs will render them more likeable and well-respected within society. If these people are unable to bear children, form romantic attachments or indulge in 'game' playing, they tend to blame themselves and can become extremely unhappy as a result.

Placed in the second: Fifth house matters become serious, financial or possessive concerns. The subject either enjoys spending money on romantic attachments and children, or sees these commitments as financially consuming. Money can be earned through children, love affairs and creative outlets, but the subject tends to view his creative endeavours purely in the light of their financial success, and may not be interested in creating anything unless it can be of material value. Children and loved ones may be viewed as possessions and there is a tendency for an over-protective attitude to be adopted by the subject.

Placed in the third: Pleasure and social interaction occur mainly through communication with relatives, siblings, neighbours and casual friends – all of whom appreciate the subject's company and lively manner of expression. The subject enjoys talking or writing about children, romantic attachments and creative outlets even though he may find the same situations uninteresting on a personal or practical level. This person does not enjoy 'lone' creative activities or single-minded attachments. To him, the fun is in being with others who can stimulate his interest.

Placed in the fourth: Children are considered as important extensions of the home. This person might say that 'a home is not a home without children.' The subject's romantic instincts become more apparent when undertaken within the confines of his own home. In fact, all fifth house activities tend to flourish when undertaken within the private environment of the subject's home. The subject may seek approval from one of his parents (usually the father) concerning love attachments and the procreation of children.

Placed in the sixth: This person likes to enjoy his work, and will do much to make it pleasurable and creative. Workmates and associates appreciate his 'fun-loving' company. Romantic attachments formed within the working environment appeal to the native's need to combine work with pleasure. Children may be introduced into the work situation and this is therefore an excellent position for mothers who seek employment where a crêche is provided. The subject's children may eventually be brought into the work situation, and business partnerships can be formed.

Placed in the seventh: The subject tends to regard all romantic attachments as possible permanent relationships. Casual affairs and flirtations do not interest him in the slightest, and he is quite capable of assessing the other person for marital potential before embarking on a courtship. Children may be viewed as being an essential component of the marriage even though the subject lacks strong parental instincts. Marriage seems to trigger the subject's need for creativity and sporting endeavours, but he will expect his partner to be just as enthralled as himself.

Placed in the eighth: This is a powerful, intense placement for deep emotional and physical relationships. Fifth house matters are expressed in a very serious, probing manner. Casual relationships are lifted into the realms of all-consuming passion. Sex is not only enjoyed, but revered and analysed in depth. Children may not be actively desired, but when they do enter into the subject's life he is in danger of becoming over-emotional and highly zealous of his offspring. Females with this position tend to become absorbed in conception, pregnancy and birth rather than the child itself. All forms of creative and sporting outlets may be undertaken as a means of eliminating excessive sexual energy.

Placed in the ninth: This is a harmonious combination which enhances the subject's popularity. Higher learning, religion, philosophy and long-distance travel are undertaken in a pleasurable and sociable manner. Even the most serious of studies will be imbued with the subject's own brand of creativity and fun. This person believes that spiritual aspirations and serious studies should be undertaken lightly with an obligation towards social interaction. The subject may feel that he can 'learn' a great deal by raising a family, or becoming romantically involved. At heart he is a serious person, who desires to expand his mind, but cannot bear to be regarded as an impassioned scholar.

Placed in the tenth: Creative outlets, sporting activities and romantic attachments are readily utilized within the subject's career. Very often the subject will be totally unconcerned with fifth house matters unless they can further his career aims and ambitions. If a game of squash played with his boss will help him to achieve promotion then this person will ensure that he becomes an expert in the sport. Romantic attachments must be decorative, useful and socially graceful. The raising of a family may be regarded as a booster to the subject's ego and career fulfilment. The subject is certainly proud of his offspring and desires that they follow on in his footsteps regarding career.

Placed in the eleventh: Fifth house concerns become important to the individual when he relates to friends and group activities. Although he is not usually endowed with a paternal nature, he may be genuinely fond of his friends' offspring and treat them with great kindness and respect. He may become involved in group activities which maintain an element of childish activity, for in his heart this subject still sees himself as a child, and tends to project these immature qualities onto his friends. He is, however, fun to be with and always 'game for a laugh'. It is important to this person that his friends approve of any romantic attachments he forms. He does not really enjoy casual relationships but is prepared to let his friends think that he does in order to gain their admiration. He prefers to indulge in sporting or creative activities with a friend rather than on his own.

Placed in the twelfth: This person possesses very deep, hidden motives regarding all fifth house matters. Secret liasions which remain undetected for a long time can easily develop. The subject does not feel able to enjoy himself in an open, honest manner. Many of his creative and romantic instincts may be acted out in the unconscious or imagination, and he may dream about achievements and love affairs which never actually materialize. The subject's attitude towards children is difficult to define, for he keeps his paternal instincts under close lock and key. Children may be denied or present problems in the form of hospitalization or institutionalization. Women with this placement often declare a desire for children, yet many unconsciously deny conception because they are afraid of the practical responsibilities that children incur. For this person, to dream of being a loving parent is infinitely better than actually becoming one.

THE SIXTH HOUSE

An empty sixth house does not signify a lack of work, poor health or a disregard for animals. It does, however indicate an acceptance of all sixth house matters. A subject with no planets in this area often possesses a stronger constitution than a person with planets here. This is especially the case when the subject also possesses a void in the twelfth house. Ironic though it may be, a person with planets in the sixth is likely to worry or be over-concerned about his health, whereas the subject with an empty sixth house who cares little about health matters very often reaps the benefits of being a naturally healthier individual.

It is extremely important to study the second house (money) and the tenth house (career and ambition) when analysing an empty sixth house. In order to earn money or be successful within a chosen career, hard work is normally required. A person with an empty sixth house can actually appear to be a workaholic if he is motivated by strong second or tenth house planets. It is only when all three houses are empty that one can say with relative safety that the subject is not overly concerned with work and the material gains of life. It is often the case, however, that a person with an empty sixth house and a strong tenth house will usually succeed in reaching the top of his chosen career without appearing to have worked too hard.

Ruler of Empty Sixth

Placed in the first: The subject enjoys projecting a healthy, hard-working image, and may receive much credit for work that he has not actually completed. He may possess much knowledge about health and nutrition but rarely put this knowledge into practice when relating to himself, because he secretly finds it rather boring. Animals are attracted to him, and he is able to put on a great show of affection for them, even though he inwardly finds many animals distasteful or dirty. This person is highly critical of his own personality and will want to be seen to do the right thing.

Placed in the second: Wherever there is a chance of gaining on a financial level, the subject is willing to work hard – or at least appear to be doing so. Work is important purely in terms of financial rewards and the gaining of possessions. The subject's health can fluctuate dramatically if his earning capacity is not stretched to the limit. With this placement there is a strong potential for the subject to earn money from animals in some manner. He is also able to gain financially through health and dietary concerns.

Placed in the third: Much short-distance daily travel is undertaken with this position. The subject enjoys communication and travelling during working hours, and will endeavour to prove to relatives, siblings and neighbours how much he values movement and change in his daily life. A steady, monotonous routine job is certainly not ideal for this person: if shut away for more than a day or two his health is likely to suffer.

Placed in the fourth: This is the ideal position for working from home – anything from the subject's own business empire to the mundane task of typing addresses on envelopes. Providing the work is carried out in the subject's own home environment he will be basically happy. Sometimes the subject can become ultra-sensitive and emotional about working conditions and can only feel secure when operating from home. Health concerns are studied in private, and if the subject becomes ill, very few people will know about it. Animals or pets in the home also add to the subject's sense of identity and innate need for security.

Placed in the fifth: The subject's fifth house requirements are rendered more practical and serious by the presence of the sixth house ruler. Work and health matters are readily integrated into the social life. To others it may appear that the 'fun' has been eliminated, but the subject derives great pleasure from working hard at his creative endeavours and carefully planning his social activities. Although the subject is totally unconcerned about his own health conditions he is likely to worry unduly about the health concerns of his children or loved ones. He may give them pets as gifts.

Placed in the seventh: Work and health situations are brought into the relationship area. The subject may saturate, or even burden his partner with his needs in this respect. The partner often works for the subject, or helps him in some way with his work, and it is not uncommon for the partner to be the 'power behind the throne'. The subject is very dependent upon his relationship(s) and is able to extract much service from them.

Placed in the eighth: This is a complex placement wherein the subject may become overzealous about his work situation in order to help him hide or forget his intense emotional and physical responses within relationships. The subject will work hard in order to receive from others – whether it be their money, their possessions, their emotions or their sexual responses. There is often an element of shrewd analytical appraisal about this position. The subject is likely to inherit a business or gain substantially through his workmates.

Placed in the ninth: The subject enjoys working hard at his studies and takes them very seriously. He communicates in a broad, philosophical manner about all matters relating to work or health and considers that he can learn a great deal about life and help himself by tackling work situations openly and expansively. His approach to long-distance travel is analytical, critical and serious. He is often involved in a work situation which requires much travel and/or study.

Placed in the tenth: When the ruler of the sixth is placed here, the subject is extremely ambitious, and will work very hard to achieve the high targets he sets for himself. Matters relating to health, service and animals are all raised into the career area, therefore rendering this a very suitable position for veterinary surgeons, zoo-keepers, doctors, nutritionists, and so on. The subject is able to reach the top in whatever he attempts, not only through his working capacity but through his shrewd, analytical abilities.

Placed in the eleventh: The subject prefers to work with friends or become involved in a working capacity within group activities. The type of work is relatively unimportant in comparison to the company he keeps whilst working. He enjoys social activity and much casual communication with many people and is therefore not happy when left to his own devices in any work situation. He finds pleasure in communicating about health or work matters with his friends and is solicitous of their well-being.

Placed in the twelfth: Although the sixth and the twelfth houses have much in common, especially when relating to health matters, this is not necessarily an easy placement for the ruler of the sixth. Work and health matters can be kept secret or hidden from the public eye and the subject may be reluctant to divulge information about them. He is, however, very capable of uncovering other people's motives and feelings concerning these matters. He may plan and plot behind the scenes but find it difficult to bring his schemes into action. At times he may feel oppressed by work and health matters and feel that he is sacrificing his true needs in order to feel of use and service in his work. There is a dark, secretive side to his nature which he struggles to analyse and keep under strict control.

THE SEVENTH HOUSE

When the seventh house is occupied it brings to the subject a need for companionship and permanent partnerships. An unoccupied seventh house does not deny these needs or the occurrence of lasting relationships but it does inject the subject with a strong desire for independence of expression within relationships. These are the people who like to formulate their own interests and lead much of their life separate from their spouse. When the fifth and the eighth houses are also void, the subject may find it difficult or undesirable to form any kind of relationship.

There is rarely a set pattern with this area unoccupied. I have seen many charts where the subject has not married at all, but just as many – if not more – where the subject has married two or three times. A mutable sign (Gemini, Virgo, Sagittarius or Pisces) on the cusp of the seventh is far more likely to indicate more than one marriage or partnership, whether the house be occupied or not. Fixed signs (Taurus, Leo, Scorpio and Aquarius) on the cusp represent loyalty and rigid attitudes concerning the partner, and therefore subjects with these signs on the seventh are reluctant to dispense with relationships once formed. Cardinal signs (Aries, Cancer, Libra and Capricorn), seem to provide a split in attitudes – Aries and Libra being extremely enthusiastic and liable to rush in where angels fear to tread, and then tire or lose interest quickly, whereas Cancer and Capricorn are much more cautious when forming attachments and can hang on indefinitely to an outworn relationship. All four signs, however, know what they want and will push to achieve their desires in this area.

The point to remember is that subjects with unoccupied seventh houses do not actually need lasting relationships, and are therefore more likely to avoid the issue, or readily escape from unhappy situations. Exceptions can occur, however, when Libra or the planet Venus are strongly represented in the birth chart.

Wherever the ruler of the seventh is placed is the area in which the subject seeks fulfilment from a relationship.

Love is not always the ultimate aim in this respect.
People marry for all sorts of reasons – home, children,
money, ambition and so on. The ruler of an empty seventh should be examined very closely when the subject
is contemplating committing himself to a lasting relationship.

Ruler of Empty Seventh

Placed in the first: This person finds it somewhat difficult
to relate to his partner's individuality and separate needs.
In his heart he longs to meet that special someone who
will be able to relate to him totally – perhaps even emanate his own personality. The subject often expects too
much of a partner, especially in the way of co-operation
and loyalty, yet his own desire for independence and
freedom remain vitally important to him. He will be
attracted by people who think, look and act like himself.

Placed in the second: The subject can gain materially
through the partner. This could be a somewhat mercen-
ary position if the subject's chart reveals too much need
for financial gain. The partner may have many ideas on
how the subject can earn money and acquire possessions.
The subject readily accepts his partner's help and can
become very possessive about his relationship(s). A partner may be viewed as an 'accessory' rather than as an
individual in his own right.

Placed in the third: The subject enjoys communicating and
undergoing short-distance travel with his partner, who
should be lively, chatty and versatile and able to offer
much in the way of variable daily activity. The subject
will expect his partner to relate in a friendly manner
towards all the relatives and neighbours who tend to be
an integral part of his lifestyle. The subject will readily
listen, learn and absorb his partner's knowledge and then
reassemble the matter in order to express it in his own
fashion.

Placed in the fourth: Home becomes a crucial factor with this placement. The subject tends to form relationships with those who can provide him with security and a firm base upon which to settle down. He enjoys being with the partner in the home, and will do all he can to maintain a strong, comfortable home environment for himself and for his partner. Because the subject sees his partner as part of the home, should the actual abode be forfeited, then the partnership could be in danger of floundering.

Placed in the fifth: Romance, children and fun are the vital requirements for this person when settling into a permanent relationship. Providing the partner can provide all these essentials the subject will be happy and fulfilled, but all too often, after the children appear, the subject finds himself weighed down with duties and responsibilities that make it difficult for the relationship to continue on a loving, romantic level. Disenchanted, the subject is liable to seek his pleasure elsewhere. This is not a good position for fidelity within marriage unless fixed signs are on the cusp of the seventh and generally dominate the chart.

Placed in the sixth: Working relationships are common with this placement. The subject enjoys sharing work and health matters with his partner, but expects his partner to show enthusiasm and respect for his working environment. Animals and/or pets are shared and considered to be important to the well-being of the relationship. The subject may be over-critical of his partner and extract much in the way of service and help.

Placed in the eighth: The strong sexual and emotional needs of the subject compel him to seek a partner who can provide these requirements. If the fourth and fifth houses are also empty he may desire little else from a relationship other than sexual compatibility and/or financial support. This position indicates that the subject will always receive from the partner in some manner. In a very powerful chart this placement could suggest a subject who commands complete power over his partner.

Placed in the ninth: The subject appreciates his partner's knowledge and philosophies in life even though he possesses his own distinctive viewpoints about these matters. Often the partner has much to teach the subject about higher learning and the spiritual aspirations of life. The subject enjoys the companionship of his partner while travelling, but will expect the partner to comply with his wishes as to destination and means of travel. If the eighth house is also empty, this placement could lack emotional and physical attunement but add much camaraderie.

Placed in the tenth: The partner may be put on a pedestal and regarded as a status symbol. The subject enjoys publicity and admiration and feels that this can be enhanced if his partner is also a willing showpiece. It is vital that the subject can feel proud of his spouse, and to this end he will not be ashamed to exploit her abilities and talents. Although the seventh house is empty the subject may strongly desire a successful, fulfilling relationship and strive very hard to achieve this aim, but it is often difficult for the subject to view his partner as an individual.

Placed in the eleventh: With this placement it is vital that the partner is also a friend to the subject. Platonic and highly spiritual relationships can develop when the ruler of the seventh is placed here, especially when the eighth and/or fifth houses are also empty. The subject needs to communicate and socialize and it therefore becomes an important issue that his partner is able to join in and feel at ease with his large circle of friends. The subject expects his partner to help him with any group activity commitments.

Placed in the twelfth: As with most twelfth house connections this position is rarely easy to express. The subject possesses unconscious needs and anxieties which he unintentionally offloads onto his partner. This is also a very secretive, behind-the-scenes placement in which the subject seems to prefer to keep his partner under lock and key. If the relationship is to succeed, the partner must be willing to sacrifice many of her own needs and acquiesce in the subject's wishes. Sometimes the subject harbours a psychological problem which makes it difficult for him to love openly and be proud of his spouse. The essence of this problem is often unconsciously projected onto the partner, where it is capable of engendering illness, trauma and resentment in the partner.

THE EIGHTH HOUSE

Because the eighth is such a closed-in, highly controlled area of life which rarely surfaces above-ground, voids in this house do not immediately shine forth as obvious lacks. It is usually true to say that a person possessing a strong eighth house, is highly sexed, highly secretive and somewhat cunning in nature with a knack of receiving love, money or possessions from others. Their emotional and physical needs are very powerful but often difficult to satisfy, partly because eighth house sexual needs are very much more spiritually engendered than the playful requirements of the fifth house or the animal instincts of the second. Theoretically, therefore, a subject with no planets in the eighth, has little or no need for this type of all-consuming love and possession, and little desire to accumulate wealth or belongings through the resources of others. The acute intensity and profound depth of the eighth house are lacking, and if fifth house planets, the sign of Scorpio and the planets Pluto and Mars are also weak then there may be little incentive to develop any strong physical attachments.

Wherever the ruler of the sign on the cusp is placed is the area in which all eighth house matters are brought out into the open (or possibly pushed further into the background, as is the case when the ruler is placed in the fourth or the twelfth).

Ruler of Empty Eighth

Placed in the first: The intensity, depth and resourceful-
ness of the eighth house sits uncomfortably in the open,
expressive façade of the first house. The subject feels
impelled to project himself in a powerful, magnetically
or sexually charged manner which may belie his more
temperate inner qualities of expression. The results of
this combination are often ambiguous. The subject may
become a venerated leader, especially where the opposite
sex is concerned, yet be disliked or even feared for his
apparent lack of simplicity, charm and balance. This is
not an easy position and whatever planets and signs are
involved there will always be an element of the planet
Mars apparent within this person's outer demeanour.

Placed in the second: The subject places much value upon
earning money, and on financial security, which is seemingly enhanced by this placement. The second and eighth
houses complement one another – therefore when the
ruler of the eighth is placed here the subject has much
to gain from others concerning second house matters.
The discerning faculties of the eighth house add insight,
courage and determination to second house affairs.
Sexual and emotional attitudes are relegated to a materialistic level, and there is some danger of the subject
decrying the spiritual qualities of love in favour of crude
or bestial sensuality.

Placed in the third: This placement is somewhat similar to
the ruler of the eighth being in the first. It is, however,
more communicative and less likely to produce powerful
leadership qualities. All eighth house matters are brought
well into the open by the subject, who enjoys conversing
on a profound level about sexuality, emotions, birth,
death and financial concerns. The subject may also possess a talent for writing and teaching on these subjects.
Short journeys and contacts with relatives and neighbours are often instigated through eighth house matters
– for example due to his innate interest in procreation,

the subject may make himself indispensable in some way during the birth of a relative.

Placed in the fourth: Eighth house concerns are kept confined to the home area, and the subject can be very cagey about his views in this respect. The subject is highly sexed, sensitive and emotional, but finds difficulty in expressing these qualities outside the security of his home environment. Public displays of sexuality are strictly taboo (unless the sign of Scorpio, or the planets Pluto and Mars are in an open, prominent position). The subject is liable to receive homes and/or possessions from others and therefore the inheritance of property or family heirlooms is very likely. I have noted several cases of females with this placement who, despite public pressure, have been determined to give birth to their children within their own homes.

Placed in the fifth: The subject regards all romantic attachments in a serious, full-blooded manner, and is determined to enjoy life to the full. This position enhances the conception and production of children, particularly within a female's chart, and often denotes a large family. The subject could become obsessed with the bearing and raising of children. Sexual pleasure is extremely important and if not satisfied with his partner's responses the subject is fully capable of seeking fulfilment elsewhere.

Placed in the sixth: The deep, impenetrable waters of the eighth house are projected into the mundane areas of work and health. The subject therefore attacks his work in an indomitable manner and finds it difficult to relax or communicate within his work environment in an easygoing, friendly manner. In-depth analysis, psychology, health and nutrition are all areas of work which the subject may find challenging and exciting. Sexual matters are enmeshed into sixth house activities and the subject enjoys physical relationships which emanate from his work environment. A typical positive occupation for this person would be a gynaecologist, whereas a typical negative occupation would be working as a whore's pimp!

Placed in the seventh: The subject strongly desires a deep, permanent relationship which is founded very much upon sexual proclivity, but which is also highly communicative and united in all areas of life. Sometimes the subject can be extremely demanding within a relationship. Partner's financial resources and possessions are regarded as his own, and there is a powerful need for this person to feel totally loved and one hundred per cent committed. There are no half measures here.

Placed in the ninth: As with all the positive houses (first, third, fifth, seventh, ninth and eleventh), the affairs of the eighth house are once again brought very much out into the open. The subject enjoys studying or debating upon deep, analytical matters of a sexual or financial nature and is usually very broad-minded regarding the practical application of such concerns. He enjoys practising what he preaches and is a great believer in truth at any cost. There could be much physical or emotional attachment to foreign lands, their people and their cultures, and a strong possibility of vibrant, passionate relationships being formed with people of foreign birth or descent.

Placed in the tenth: The ruler of the eighth placed in this house seems to add confidence, determination and intense concentration on career matters. This person takes himself very seriously and is very likely to succeed in life. Sexual and financial matters are openly discussed in order to further career aims, but inwardly the subject might doubt or be over-sensitive about all that he declares to be right. On a psychological level he may view his career as his lover, and pursue it with idealistic passion and obsessive intensity. The actual career might be centred upon eighth house objectives.

Placed in the eleventh: The subject enjoys touching, and making emotional demands upon his friends. He may find it difficult to form purely casual friendships. Those in whom he places his trust are usually also those from whom he desires much response. When the overriding physical demands are transmuted, however, the subject is capable of powerful spiritual friendships in which he gives all that he has. In contrast, however, on a negative level the subject may be excited by group sex and unusual emotional or sexual stimulation. The eighth house is renowned for its financial acumen, so therefore this is a good placement for the subject to be involved with the accounts or treasury of a group activity.

Placed in the twelfth: This placement is so deep that it can be virtually unfathomable. As with all twelfth house combinations the influence can be expressed on the highest or lowest plane of existence. The subject's emotional and sexual responses can be inhibited through excessive shyness, or perverted with a profound love and need of secrecy. Sexual instincts could lead the subject into sorrow, trauma and crime on an extreme negative level, but on the highest of levels this is the person who subjugates all sexual desires and becomes a monk, or even a saint. Other people's money, possessions or inheritance could come to hand through institutions, hospitals, prisons or charities. With a lack of second house planets also, this person cares little about the material concerns of life.

THE NINTH HOUSE

The areas of life represented by the ninth house are very far-reaching and expansive, both on a mental and physical level. It is rarely of great consequence therefore to find a void within this area. If both the third and the ninth are empty it may be somewhat difficult for the subject to expand his mind or intellect to any degree at all, but the lack of planets also decrees that the subject finds it unnecessary to improve his mental stimulation.

People with planets in the ninth house are often very restless, enquiring individuals. Those with voids lack this volubility (unless the third house, the signs of Gemini and Sagittarius, and the planet Mercury are strong). Travelling is not an important issue. The subject usually finds it easy to accept or reject whatever the ninth house offers.

Ruler of Empty Ninth

Placed in the first: This is a harmonious, fiery placement which adds a touch of *joie de vivre* and optimism to any ascending sign. The subject is relaxed and more able to express his outer personality when the expansive ninth house ruler is placed here. He enjoys projecting himself as a learned and well-travelled individual – which in reality is rarely the case – but most people fall hook, line and sinker for his lively, enthusiastic tales about his many adventures. The subject is usually popular despite his somewhat false exterior.

Placed in the second: All ninth house matters are viewed on a very practical, materialistic level. If the subject feels that extra learning or study can benefit him financially then he will make the necessary efforts to improve himself. Travel is preferably undertaken for financial gain, as is earning a living abroad. The subject may express values and opinions which are very expansive and philosophical, but he will tend to tie them in with material gains or needs.

Placed in the third: All forms of travel, learning, philosophies and religions become mundane within the eyes of the subject. He enjoys relegating higher-level and spiritual pursuits to a lower, personal level which he is more easily able to understand. Much travel, both short- and long-distance is undertaken in an effort to broaden his personal horizons. He enjoys passing on his knowledge to relatives and neighbours. He may spend much time with them, some of it on journeys.

Placed in the fourth: Unless there are indications in the chart which decree otherwise, this person really prefers not to travel to foreign lands at all. He is specifically a 'home-bird'. He may enjoy reading, or watching television programmes concerning foreign lands and cultures, from within his home environment. Studying and learning via postal courses, videos or cassettes are also more popular means of learning. On the surface it often appears that this person possesses little desire for intellectual stimulation, but he is capable of surprising those who know him well with his vast amount of knowledge – all of which has been acquired from the comfort of his favourite armchair!

Placed in the fifth: This is an overt, pleasure-seeking placement which adds to the popularity of the subject. Ninth house concerns are treated very personally and socially. The subject tends to form romantic attachments with persons of foreign birth or descent or with those of a completely different culture from his own. He is also stimulated by highly intelligent, intellectual or spiritual people who can converse widely on their chosen field of study. This person is an adventurer in every sense of the word and he values the company of those who are prepared to seek excitement with him.

Placed in the sixth: The subject needs expansive communicative outlets within his work environment. He does not desire to travel overmuch himself, but enjoys working with the travels and studies of others. This is a good placement for travel agents, college principals and course organisers. The subject works well with people of foreign birth or descent and often finds himself employed with people of varying nationalities. All matters connected with travel, study and foreign lands are in some way beneficial to the health and well-being of the subject.

Placed in the seventh: Travel and learning are only truly enjoyed when the subject is accompanied or assisted by his partner. The subject can truly believe in the adventurous, expansive spirit of the ninth house when he is given support. Often the partner is of foreign birth or descent and either very wise, philosophical and learned, or of an extremist religious group. It is more usual with this

position, however, for the partner to live in the subject's
country of birth, rather than vice versa.

Placed in the eighth: Although the subject does not openly
express an interest in ninth house concerns, he is very
likely to study them deeply in secret, or in an underhand
manner. These people make excellent spies, undercover
agents or detectives. They are capable of learning, and
utilizing any ninth house religion or philosophy for their
own means. Passionate or obsessive relationships with
persons of foreign birth or descent are likely to occur.
The subject is stimulated on an emotional and physical
level by anybody who is vastly different from himself.
He may be involved in some kind of financial dealings
with people from foreign lands.

Placed in the tenth: This is the position of the person who
travels and learns incessantly for the sake of improving
his career status. He may be involved in business partnerships with people of foreign birth or descent, or of
an entirely different religion to his own. Although not
inherently a learned person, the subject is easily able to
convince others that he has had a good education and
is capable of any task placed before him. Although this
combination is rarely relaxed or easy it does seem to
bring success to the subject's career.

Placed in the eleventh: This placement confers upon the
subject a highly active, sociable and friendly disposition.
He enjoys the company of all those who are able to
express themselves freely within their chosen religion or
philosophy. He is likely to participate in many group
activities which involve ninth house matters. Foreign
communities, especially those involving humane or eco-
logical causes, interest him greatly. This person possesses
many friends and is well-liked, even though he may be
somewhat opinionated or over-zealous at times.

Placed in the twelfth: The subject feels unable to explore
the higher potentials of his mind, which is, at all times,
highly active and imaginative, but there is a blockage,

which can be of psychological or karmic origin. Study or learning is either undertaken in secret or completely sacrificed in favour of other matters. This person finds it difficult to communicate on an open level, although strong placements in the third house can do much to mitigate the effect. He does not relate well to people of foreign birth or descent, but may be thrown into contact with them through institutions, hospitals or big organisations. If, and when, the subject manages to reach the positive level of this difficult placement, he may achieve much through sacrificing his own needs and turning to religious or spiritual pursuits.

THE TENTH HOUSE

An anomaly arises when endeavouring to categorise the tenth house, for although it is a passive (negative) area naturally ruled by the somewhat shy, insecure sign of Capricorn and the serious, fearful planet Saturn, those with planets in this house usually exhibit extroverted, self-assured qualities and a strong desire to come under the public eye in some way. One must assume therefore, that this overt confidence is often a very convincing cover for the many insecurities which lurk beneath the surface. Ambition and recognition are pawns to be used in order that the subject can respect himself.

Upbringing and parental influences are strong for any tenth house person and usually have much bearing upon the subject's outer demeanour and needs for career fulfilment.

An empty tenth house can at first appear to generate a lack of ambition or motivation, and an inability to reach the top in a chosen profession. This assumption is often a misconception. Although people without planets here do not struggle to attain dizzy heights, providing they are naturally gifted they can automatically gain recognition, success and fame. As with all empty houses, the karmic implications are that the subject has earned the right not to have to struggle within these areas of life. Void tenth house subjects will accept what transpires on a career level and will rarely push to achieve greater heights, whereas a person with planets in this house will always be striving to achieve more and more, until eventually they stretch just that little bit too far, topple over, and come tumbling down the other side of the mountain to settle in an undignified heap at the bottom, whereupon the undeterred subject will pick himself up and start all over again. These rises and falls do not happen in the lives of those with no planets in the tenth. There is far less likelihood of dramatic success, and therefore they rarely fall.

I have noticed that when the tenth house is occupied by one of the three outer planets, Uranus, Neptune and Pluto, the rise and fall situation becomes more prominent and extremely fateful, especially when the planet is tightly angular or conjunct the Midheaven (this can occur in any of the four houses from the eighth to the eleventh when using the equal house system, which I prefer). Extreme rises to fame can occur with traumatic, sad or unlikely endings occurring. It is not, therefore, as fortunate as it may seem to possess planets in the tenth house. The person with a void here is liable to lead a more settled and therefore less stressful lifestyle.

An empty tenth house also points to an independence from one of the parents, usually the mother. Whereas those with planets here tend to want to please or emulate the mother in some way, a lack here often indicates a person who is very unlikely to follow in the mother's footsteps or be influenced by her needs, aims and desires. Sometimes a void here can indicate a lack of feeling or concern regarding the designated parent.

When analysing the tenth for career potential, always check whether planets are posited in the sixth house or the second house. One or both of these houses occupied might force the void tenth house subject to aim higher than he would do otherwise.

The characteristics of tenth house planets are swiftly recognized within the personality of the subject. A lack of tenth house renders the subject more difficult to analyse, especially regarding career potential.

Ruler of Empty Tenth

Placed in the first: This person oozes authority, power and personality, and can give the impression of being extremely ambitious, determined or ruthless. In reality, however, the subject lacks the drive to push himself forward and tends to rely heavily upon his magnetic personality to accomplish results. He is liable to achieve positions of power, popularity or fame which he does not truly need or desire. He tends to express himself very much as a career-orientated person and may therefore appear to be somewhat self-absorbed.

Placed in the second: Career is relegated to material and financial matters. The subject is ambitious, or even greedy for money and for the recognition which he considers will be showered upon him as a wealthy person. The subject can become possessive regarding career situations and is in danger of not seeing the wood for the trees, especially if he is aware that there is something to be gained on a material level. Where money or material requisites are concerned the subject will push, and work hard to achieve status and power, but he rarely possesses the innate drive, personality or authority that a person with planets in the tenth seems to engender.

Placed in the third: The subject enjoys communicating and much mundane travel within his career. This is an ideal placement for success in careers such as teaching, selling, lecturing or writing. The subject does not necessarily aim very high in these endeavours but will often have success thrust upon him. The subject is very willing to help his relatives to progress on their own career paths, and it is highly possible that he may work with them in some manner.

Placed in the fourth: This placement reduces the quotient of extroverted qualities which the subject may possess. The career is brought down into the area of home and is hidden from view. The subject enjoys most home-making pursuits and feels more relaxed if he is able to work from home. Suitable careers are domestic work, small private one-man businesses, private catering, hotel work and estate agents. This placement often confers that one of the parents (usually the mother) has taken on the role of both parents, and is able to exert much influence over the subject. She may help to further his career.

Placed in the fifth: The subject attaches more importance to his creative endeavours than to his actual career. He may try to combine the two, or ensure that whatever career he has chosen enables him to express his strong creative talents. Romantic attachments and children are also extremely important to the individual, but they may be viewed as ambitious projects or obsessive aims. The subject may be more ambitious for his loved ones and children than himself. This is a good placement for careers in sport, leisure, entertainment and child-minding.

Placed in the sixth: The nature of the work and the fulfil-ment gained from the work environment are more impor-tant to the native than career prospects. The subject is able to formulate a career from any job which he enjoys, however mundane. If there are no second house planets to encourage financial requirements, the subject may be content to work for very little reward and possibly become a workaholic. The subject guards his health very seriously and can become highly motivated by health matters – a negative attitude resulting in hypochondria – a positive attitude indicative of a career in the medical, welfare, caring or healing professions.

Placed in the seventh: The partner is put on a pedestal and regarded as a token of achievement. The subject finds great satisfaction in helping his partner to succeed, either through status, career or public recognition. All his career energies are channelled through his partner and he appears to be a very altruistic soul, but he is in danger of becoming obsessed with his partner's accomplishments without really being able to evaluate her innermost needs and capabilities.

Placed in the eighth: In a similar vein to when the ruler of the tenth is placed in the fourth (and the twelfth) this placement pushes the qualities of the tenth house underground and to a certain degree renders them inaccessible. The eighth house, however, is the strongest of the three water houses and nobody with this placement should be underestimated. The subject may seem quiet and unassuming, but underneath he is surprisingly ambitious, determined and resourceful. Career aims are kept in check until the right moment for advancement. Any careers requiring intense physical or mental probing such as psychiatry, detective-work, mining and sub-aqua diving, are suitable for this person.

Placed in the ninth: The subject needs to formulate a career within communication, religious activities, languages, foreign studies, higher-level teaching, lecturing, or travel, in order to feel at one with himself. He is not ambitious but is capable of great advancement in life due to his expansive, philanthropic expression, and/or highly intellectual mind. The subject may be parted from his mother (or both parents) at a relatively early age, and live in a foreign country. It is one of his most fervent aims, however, to reunite himself with mother, and this normally occurs when the mother leaves her country of birth to live with the subject.

Placed in the eleventh: Friends and group activities are significantly more important to the subject than his career, but he will somehow manage to combine the separate facets of his life. The subject is ambitious for his friends and will do everything he can to help them. He is likely to take on positions of responsibility in group situations, taking his duties very seriously, perhaps devoting more time to them than to his work. This placement would suit a Personnel Officer, a Youth Club organiser or any career involving major group participation and human causes.

Placed in the twelfth: Career aims and objectives are hidden and obscure. The subject can find it immensely difficult to choose a career and stick to it. Deep-rooted insecurities and problems of self-expression often beset him. Sometimes the subject is his own worst enemy, allowing his imagination to get the better of him, and wasting his energies in merely dreaming of being famous and well-loved. If the sixth and/or second houses are emphasised in the natal chart, much may be overcome and achieved with this placement – otherwise there is a strong indication of little being accomplished. The subject is happier when involved in a career which pushes him behind the scenes. Hospital, institution and charity work is particularly suitable for this enigmatic individual.

THE ELEVENTH HOUSE

Voids in this area are indicative of strong-minded, capable individuals who do not need the support of close friends and group activities. Without the benefit of planets in either the third or the seventh they may also be extreme loners who find it unnecessary to communicate at all.

There are, however, many levels of friendship – a fact which can render it somewhat difficult to categorize a person's needs in this respect. The closest, most intimate friendships are those relating to the seventh house. Children tend to develop seventh house friendships far more than adults do, because their immaturity allows them to accept the intimate stage of a friendship without becoming enmeshed in physical and emotional situations. Some adults do, however, form extremely close seventh house friendships which are purely platonic and not dependent upon an intimate relationship. These are usually the people with at least one personal planet posited in the seventh house.

The least involved area when categorizing friendships, is the third house. Acquaintances, neighbours and very casual friends fall under the domain of the highly communicative house. Third house friendships represent a need for communication of all kinds, but they do not encourage dependency, warmth or closeness.

Eleventh house friendship falls somewhere midway between the seventh and the third house requirements, and is therefore indicative of a more natural type of friendship. Some element of trust, closeness and support is normally required by those with planets here, but not in the over-dependent manner of the seventh house person.

Most people without planets in the eleventh do possess at least one planet in the third or seventh, and therefore a total lack of friendships rarely exists, but those with a void in the eleventh house are rarely group-orientated, and will either choose their friends very discriminatingly (seventh house support) or indiscriminantly (third house support).

Ruler of Empty Eleventh

Placed in the first: This person is very much aware of his or her own personality and likes to be seen to have plenty of friends. The support and comradeship of many friends helps the subject to express himself more easily, and he is therefore usually a popular person, despite the tendency to use his friends for his own needs. Although the subject does not necessarily enjoy the limelight, he does covetously desire that group activities are centred around himself – otherwise he quickly loses interest.

Placed in the second: The subject receives much support from his friends, especially where material matters are concerned. Friends may put forward ideas on how the subject can gain financially, or how they may be able to help him out on a practical level. The subject can be very possessive about friends and group activity concerns, though he will not normally become involved in group situations unless there is some profit to be incurred on a material level. To an outsider the subject with this placement can appear to be very self-centred in his attitudes towards the unstinting loyalty of his friends, but there are always two sides to any situation and the subject's capacity to receive allows his friends to experience the pleasure of giving.

Placed in the third: This person has many friends, especially amongst relatives and neighbours with whom he is able to communicate on a very open level. His company is highly sought for its wit and intelligence, and he enjoys entertaining his chosen circle of friends whom he regards as his subjects. He does not enjoy truly close friendships or remaining anonymous with casual group activities. He needs to talk, to communicate in a vital manner himself and is rarely able to remain in the background. He treats all his friends in an equal manner and enjoys escorting them on their daily travels.

Placed in the fourth: A quiet, tentative placement for the ruler of the eleventh which confers a certain amount of introvertism and a need for security. The subject does not express himself easily with friends (unless there is a powerful third house), but enjoys their company in his own home. These people make good hosts or hostesses once they are confident about the company they have chosen. They may be reticent to join in any group situation, but at some stage in their lives may readily agree to such activities taking place within their own home. They possess few very close friends.

Placed in the fifth: These people are generally fun-loving and sociable, but disinclined towards group activities. They prefer to provide their own entertainment rather than rely on the more structured, organized events typical of the eleventh house. They are born leaders who do not enjoy following the dictates of others, although they are easily able to disguise this fact with their pleasant, outgoing characters. Romantic attachments often develop through friendships. Friends are helpful or beneficial to the subject's children and/or creative endeavours.

Placed in the sixth: Friends and group involvement become important to the subject's work environment. He may not be naturally sociable or group-orientated but he needs the support and communication of close friends in his work situation. As much as he may enjoy the work, without the company of others he can feel dejected or unappreciated. Friends are often the source of helpful advice concerning his health or pets, and they may actually play an important role in the recovery from any illness to which he falls prey.

Placed in the seventh: The subject classifies all his friends under the one category – seventh house. He is a warm-natured, communicative individual who needs many close or even intimate friendships in order to feel fulfilled. He is basically a one-to-one person and feels insecure within groups because he cannot relate singularly to all his friends at the same time. Marriage or permanent relationships may ensue from a close friendship. It is vital that his partners also remain his friends after marriage, because this person is rarely content with one close relationship.

Placed in the eighth: Friendships are intense and serious. The subject finds it difficult to relate to others in a friendly open manner. He controls his needs and shrewdly evaluates any potential friend or group activity for their relevant worth within his life. He often prefers to keep his friends secret or well hidden, but is loyal once committed and able to exercise much authority and magnetism over the chosen few. Materially, the subject is likely to gain through his friends. Highly emotional or passionate relationships can develop through friendships.

Placed in the ninth: This is a gregarious, outgoing placement, in which the subject values friendships and group activities for the intellectual support they are able to offer. He does not desire close friendships, but enjoys the company of like-minded individuals. He is likely to be the instigator of group activities which are based upon his own interests in life. He makes many casual friends whilst travelling, and would make an excellent lay-preacher, or university professor. He can be magnanimous, grandiose or eccentric, but he is rarely disliked.

Placed in the tenth: The subject may use his friends or group activities in order to further his ambitions, but as is usually the case with these 'receptive' placements, the subject's friends are more than willing to help him out. Apart from his working colleagues, the subject possesses very few close personal friends. He is choosy about those who are allowed to associate with him, and is not averse to toadying or demeaning himself in order to achieve added status through friends or exclusive group activities.

Placed in the twelfth: Friendships are not formed easily. The subject is often shy and insecure with people he does not know well. He may develop imaginary friends in order to appease the demands made upon him by society. In reality he is a loner and is quite happy to live in his own inner world (unless the remainder of the chart is dominated by positive house placements, especially in the third or seventh). Friendships and group activities are more likely to be formed within hospitals, institutions and prisons, or through charitable work. The subject possesses very deep-rooted unconscious ideals about friendships, but is rarely able to express these views openly.

THE TWELFTH HOUSE

In view of the fact that planets (especially the five personal planets) situated in the twelfth house are rarely easy to utilize on a positive level and, when difficultly aspected, are often the root cause of severe problems in a birth chart, it is in my opinion nearly always advantageous to possess a void in this area. The exception to this is in the case of the three outer planets, which when well aspected seem to fare much better in this deep, karmically based area. Despite my extensive experience as an astrologer I have never truly managed to overcome that immediate feeling of anguish when erecting a birth chart with strong twelfth house connections, or that slight feeling of relief upon seeing the twelfth house empty. These feelings are not always warranted, because many twelfth house people seem to struggle by, and some even manage to lead positive, accomplished lives, but many more fall by the wayside, become physically or mentally ill, or just simply become lost in their thankless search for self-expression. People with voids in this area, no matter how difficult the remainder of the chart, can consider themselves lucky not to have to face the traumatic inner struggles that the twelfth house person has to endure. A void in the twelfth tends to add just a little semblance of balance to even the most imbalanced of charts.

Everybody, however, possesses a sign on the cusp of their twelfth house, and a planet to rule that sign. We all therefore have one area of our lives in which the expression of the twelfth house is stimulated to a minor degree. Although the ruler of the twelfth is usually happier when placed in the negative houses (second, fourth, sixth, eighth and tenth), it is allowed more freedom of expression when placed in the positive houses (first, third, fifth, seventh, ninth and eleventh) and thus tends to lessen the insular, inhibited qualities projected by the house.

The twelfth house also represents sorrow and sacrifice, and the house in which the ruler falls usually harbours its fair share of these properties. Often the subject feels misunderstood in this area and unable to express his finer qualities.

Ruler of Empty Twelfth

Placed in the first: One of the better placements for the ruler, especially if a personal planet is involved. The subject is rarely allowed to become morose, withdrawn or secretive, because the qualities of the twelfth house are brought to the surface for all to see. The subject may endeavour to project a 'closed book' image with much to reveal underneath, but in reality there is nothing under the cover, and the subject rarely fools anybody. An element of quietness is often added to the personality, but at least the subject is able to offload any twelfth house problems in a relatively easy manner, even though at times he feels very much maligned or misunderstood.

Placed in the second: The subject is able to incur material gains through secretive, or underhand means. Hospitals, institutions, prisons or charitable organizations could engender some source of income for the subject. This is a good placement for earning money through hospital, institutional or charitable work, although as far as the latter is concerned the subject is on the receiving end rather than the giving end. He may, therefore, seem to be in need of charity, when in fact he is usually financially secure. There could, however, be an element of self-destructiveness about the subject's handling of his finances and possessions, and self-induced losses could occur.

Placed in the third: Another placement which allows the characteristics of the twelfth house to be expressed openly and communicatively. It is not always easy, however, for the subject to express himself without emitting depressive, sorrowful or self-destructive tendencies, but he believes in speaking his mind and enjoys talking about twelfth house matters. Unless there are other planets in the third house to help alleviate the effect, he may unwittingly scare others away with his strange outlook upon life. Very often the subject finds himself involved in mundane travel and daily activity in connection with his relatives' twelfth house requirements. For instance, the subject may need to travel daily in order to care for a sick relative, or visit a neighbour in hospital.

Placed in the fourth: The 'behind the scenes' qualities of the twelfth house are very much at home when placed in the fourth. As a result, unless other planetary positions decree otherwise, the subject can become very withdrawn and remote, preferring to live a quiet, secure life in his own home. The ruler of the twelfth rarely allows a life of ease, however, and the subject may have to make many sacrifices before being given the privilege of a settled home-life. Some children with this placement grow up in a hospital or institutional environment. One of the parents (usually the father) may have been a constant source of anxiety for the subject – perhaps requiring constant care and attention or unwittingly demanding much sacrifice on the part of his child. The subject may endure many sorrows in and around the home situation throughout his life, but only a handful of close contacts will be aware of these problems.

Placed in the fifth: Although the twelfth house energies are brought out into the open, the fun-loving, competitive qualities of the fifth house are not at all compatible with twelfth house inhibitions. The subject feels obliged to bring his deeper, more introspective self to the surface, but often resents the restriction it brings to his fifth house needs. He may adore his children, take great pleasure in sporting, creative and/or competitive activities and enjoy romantic attachments, but unless there are other planets in the fifth house, all these pleasures in life are tinged with sorrow or self-destructive qualities. The subject may say or do something which he knows will bring him unhappiness, but cannot prevent himself from doing so. Sometimes the subject's children or romantic attachments will bring him into contact with hospitals, institutions or large government-run organizations.

Placed in the sixth: These two houses complement one another and therefore this is probably the best passive house for the ruler of the twelfth to occupy. Health concerns are very important and the subject enjoys working within health-related establishments. Despite his practical abilities, however, the subject is often unable to suppress the feelings of negativity, depression, inferiority and insecurity which tend to arise regularly within his daily working life and healthy living consciousness. He may feel that he has given his all to a job only to find that he is stabbed in the back by secret adversaries or underhand activities. Often it is the subject himself who is his own worst enemy in this respect, as he tends to lack communicative skills within his work environment and can project a shy, or inhibited image which is often mistaken for cold detachment.

Placed in the seventh: This is not an easy placement, despite the openness of the seventh house. Many of the subject's twelfth house inclinations are unconsciously transferred to the partner. As a result the partner may bring or cause sorrow to the subject. The subject, being unaware that it is his own projection which causes most of the problems is likely to repeat himself in any subsequent involvements. Hospitals, institutions, prisons and charities are some of the major environments which can easily constitute a major portion of the partner's life. The subject often feels that he is sacrificing his own life for the sake of his partner's well-being.

Placed in the eighth: In this position the ruler of the twelfth is likely to seek solace in underground, secretive pursuits. Just as the eighth house, the sign of Scorpio, and the planet Pluto can manifest themselves on the highest level (the phoenix) or the lowest level (the scorpion), so can the ruler of the twelfth when placed here. Strong psychic or intuitive ability is highly likely but it is up to the subject how he utilizes this powerful gift. A negative twelfth house influence overshadowing the planet(s) in the eighth could result in abuse of occult powers, or secret, unnatural sexual desires, whereas a positive twelfth house influence adds a wealth of compassion, honourable psychic intentions and healing capacity to the eighth house subject. Much of the characteristic discrepancy could be due to karmic factors. An 'old soul' with this combination is truly a good person, whereas a younger soul cannot always harness the remarkable gifts he has been given. All subjects, however, are likely to receive – either physically or emotionally from twelfth house concerns.

Placed in the ninth: Probably one of the best placements

for the ruler of the twelfth. Both houses involve religious predilections – the ninth representing the expansive, philosophical leanings, and the twelfth the fervent dedication to the belief in God. Twelfth house people can easily become sucked in by religious cults, which may possess a strongly ninth house person as their leader. The combination of the two houses can often indicate a genuinely devout person. As always, however, the negative influence of the twelfth house is rarely far from the surface and the ninth house is certainly not exempt from this influence, but it is within travel that the more self-destructive qualities are likely to occur. Hospitals, prisons and asylums are liable to enter into the subject's life whilst he is travelling. The twelfth house also rules enemies, and when the ruler is placed in the ninth, secret enemies, possibly of foreign birth or descent are likely to be brought to the surface.

Placed in the tenth: The purposeful strivings to achieve recognition by the tenth house subject can be very much watered down with this connection. Despite his powerful need to 'be' somebody, the subject feels unworthy, or unable to push himself into the limelight. The inhibited, self-destructive qualities of the twelfth house are brought out into the open and projected into his career. The rise and fall situation mentioned in relation to the tenth house can be very prominent with this placement. The subject is rarely able to express his true needs in this respect and as a result may inwardly despise himself, or his superiors for the sorrow which seems to follow him when endeavouring to achieve public recognition and respect. A career within, or involving any twelfth house sector, can be quite effective in mitigating the lesser desired contributions of the twelfth house.

Placed in the eleventh: This position can be one of the easier placements for the ruler of the twelfth. Once again the qualities of the twelfth house are forced out into the open – this time to be utilized within the sociable, humane area of the eleventh. The subject desires friendships and enjoys group situations but is not always able to express his feelings as openly as he would like. Nevertheless his need to join in is too strong to deny and his inhibitions are therefore put to one side. He is likely to become involved in all group activities which feature humane causes such as physically or mentally handicapped societies, the Samaritans, Alcoholics Anonymous, and so on. Positively, the subject is able to do much to help these people, but negatively he may unwittingly be the source of involving his friends in sorrowful situations. He strives to be popular, but he is often rejected for his efforts.

TRANSITS AND PROGRESSIONS THROUGH UNOCCUPIED HOUSES

When any progressed or transiting planets move into natally empty areas, for a time – as long as it takes for the planet to traverse the relevant house – the qualities of the specific area are highlighted and exposed. Transits and progressions are very important when they make aspects to natal planets, but when they enter an unoccupied house in a birth chart, they often have an overpowering effect upon the individual who has hitherto been very relaxed about the area in question.

TRANSITS

It is impossible for anyone not to experience at certain stages in their lives the transiting effects of planets in their unoccupied houses. All the planets from the Sun through to Saturn will enter these areas on a cyclical basis – the Moon once every twenty-eight days for a spell of approximately two and a half days, the Sun once a year for approximately thirty days. Mercury, Venus and Mars possess variable cycles but all three travel the 360 degrees of the birth chart within a timespan of two years – Mercury and Venus travelling much faster and thereby usually returning twice within this time, and occupying one sign (or one house) for a minimum span of sixteen days (Mercury) or a maximum span of almost eight months (Mars). Jupiter's twelve-year cycle ensures that it will enter all unoccupied houses during this time and stay in the area for approximately one year. Saturn's longer cycle of twenty-eight to thirty years ensures that most people will experience Saturn in their unoccupied houses for a spell of approximately two and a half years.

When considering the three outer planets, only those people who live beyond the approximate age of 84 will undergo a full Uranus return and therefore experience the galvanizing effects of this planet in all their empty houses. The very slow movement of Neptune and Pluto decrees that these two planets never complete a full cycle during any one person's lifetime – thereby ensuring that most people do not experience the effects of these planets in all of their unoccupied houses.

The transiting influence of the five personal planets, Sun, Moon, Mercury, Venus and Mars is of a temporary nature and therefore far less significant than the transiting influence of the remaining planets, Jupiter, Saturn, Uranus, Neptune and Pluto. This determinant is emphasized when planets enter unoccupied houses. Radical changes of character often become apparent immediately one of these five outer planets (especially the three outermost, Uranus, Neptune and Pluto) enter an unoccupied area in the birth chart. We have all known people who 'appear' to change their character or the course of their lives overnight. This momentous change can sometimes become an integral constituent of the subject's character even when the relevant planet has left the unoccupied house, especially with regard to the planets, Jupiter, Saturn and Pluto, which seem to have a more permanent transitory effect.

Transiting Uranus instigates drastic changes which seem to be irreversible at the time of occupancy, but the moment the seven-year cycle of this planet comes to an end, and a new area (house) of life is embarked upon, the previous cyclic changes are usually forgotten, thereby enabling the subject to return to his former lifestyle or habits if he so desires.

The transits of Neptune and Pluto are far too long not
to have any permanent effect upon the subject. The
effects of Neptune, however, are very intangible and
almost impossible to stabilize or categorize. The confus-
ing cloud which appears during a Neptune transit
quickly disperses when Neptune moves on to new territory, leaving behind a damp, soggy patch to remind us
of the chaos and disillusion it has caused by its nebulous
presence, whereas the volcanic, transforming effects of
Pluto often generate huge scars which take time to heal.
Once a subject has experienced a complete transit of
Neptune or Pluto through an unoccupied house he is
never quite the same again.

PROGRESSIONS

When analysing progressed planets in relation to unoccupied houses, the general rules of progressions apply –
only the five personal planets and sometimes Jupiter are
used – the remaining four usually moving too slowly to
form any major changes. Progressed planets work in a
similar manner to the transits of the four outermost
planets, Saturn, Uranus, Neptune and Pluto – thus they
are of great interpretative significance when moving into
an empty house. Only the Moon moves relatively quickly
– in a similar cycle to that of transiting Saturn – taking
approximately two and a half years to traverse through
one sign or house of the birth chart. (This rule only
applies when using the Equal House system. The vari-
ation in the size of houses when using most other sys-
tems of house division manifests an imbalance of cycles
within the houses of the birth chart.)

Progressed Sun takes approximately thirty years to
travel through one sign or house, and is an extremely
important factor when determining an individual's
character. A man born with the Sun in Aries becomes a
great deal more stable and settled in life when his progressed Sun enters Taurus, but may find it difficult to
adapt if there are no natal planets placed in this prag-
matic sign. Mercury, Venus and Mars all vary in the

length of time it takes them to progress 30 degrees, but Mercury's cycle is usually slightly shorter than the Sun's thirty years, while that of Venus is slightly longer. Mars can often be much longer, and in some cases, when a lengthy spell of retrograde motion occurs within a few months after the subject's birth, it will not enter another sign or house during the subject's lifetime. Jupiter can be used as the subject grows older, especially if it enters a new sign or an unoccupied house.

KARMA AND PERSONAL DEVELOPMENT

With the occurrence of transits and progressions into these empty houses, 'new' components of the character are formed and temporary karmic obligations arise. These temporary obligations can either be regarded as tests which arise as a means of discovering if we have truly learnt the lessons of previous lifetimes, or as samples of future lessons to be sustained – the latter theoretically being the most difficult to contend with due to a lack of experience or inner knowledge about the area concerned, whereas in the former case, providing the matters of the house have been learnt well, the subject should not find these transits or progressions overly difficult – just somewhat irksome. Generally speaking, an 'older soul' will have undergone more karmic lessons throughout his many lifetimes, and should therefore be more able to accept and overcome the problems presented by transits and progressions.

In the case of transiting personal planets all tests are minor and fleeting, with little overall permanent effect, but when considering the five outermost planets transits and progressions become more serious and will always demand positive action on the part of the subject. A transiting or progressed planet forming a major aspect whilst travelling through an unoccupied area will always have a devastating impact, especially if the two planets concerned do not make any contacts within the natal chart.

A person who does not experience a major transit

(Neptune, Pluto and possibly Uranus) or progression (Sun, Mercury, Venus or Mars) into an unoccupied house, is far more likely to have learnt control and composure regarding these matters during past lifetimes. The house in which the ruler of the cusp of the empty house is placed is also a minor testing ground, but this is a permanent placement and as such represents a small degree of unlearned matter.

All this extracurricular planetary activity does ensure that virtually everybody will experience changes in character, motivation and lifestyle at some stage in their lives. Those people who possess a Splash type chart shaping – wherein all the planets are dotted evenly around the chart in as many signs and houses as possible – are more able to accept change within their lives. They possess fewer unoccupied houses and less intensity of characteristics. They are highly adaptable, and enjoy applying themselves to a 'little bit of everything'. The reverse of this is exemplified in the Bundle type shaping where all the planets are confined within one-third or less of the birth chart. These people lead concentrated lives and find it difficult to adapt to the areas of life in which they have no planets – which can number between seven and nine. I have never come across a chart possessing more than nine unoccupied houses, although it is feasible for ten houses to be empty when the outer planets are grouped very close together (as they were in the very late 1980s).

As each planet enters an unoccupied house, it will instil into the subject a need to concentrate a great deal more on the area concerned. The planet engenders the type of energy required, and the sign the manner in which that energy is expended. A normally positive, outgoing person can become oversensitive, cautious and secretive if most of the transiting and progressed planets are moving through his passive houses. Likewise, the reverse situation could occur. It is consistently the planet and the relevant house which are the most important factors within transits and progressions. An unoccupied house possesses a sign on the cusp which is a constant factor from the moment of birth, but the planets come and go, each planet bringing its own unique brand of energy, as shown below.

THE SUN

By transit: Within the course of one year the Sun will have travelled through all unoccupied houses. Its effect is usually felt within mundane, daily matters, such as the need to procure a new hairstyle when it enters into the first house, or the desire to be more positive and aim towards higher achievement within a working environment as it moves into the sixth house.

By progression: Probably the most important of the progressed positions – not only as regards the house but the sign it occupies. Only when the ascending degree and the degree of the Sun are simultaneously at the very end or the very beginning of a sign do the sign and the house of the progressed Sun change at approximately the same time. For the majority of individuals these changes do not coincide, and therefore the Sun experiences two major progressed situations during its thirty-year cycle. The change of house has far more impact than the change of sign – which is felt on a more subtle level, but both are very apparent and extremely important. The active and passive influence of the signs and houses is a major concern when relating to progressed Sun. Extroverts become quiet (active to passive sign) introverts become self-assured (passive to active sign), workaholics become relationship-orientated (sixth to seventh house) or restless, hardened travellers become home-based individuals (third to fourth house). The changes are usually vast and complex with much self-adjustment required on behalf of the native. The person with planets already placed in these new areas has a head-start over the person whose Sun is moving into almost alien territory.

If the Sun immediately makes aspects upon entering this new area, the effect is even more significant. The Sun rules our inner identity – the person who we really are inside, therefore all progressed positions of the Sun indicate changes within our inner self. For instance a person born with the Sun in Leo is destined to experience the inner needs of the sign of Virgo before he reaches the age of 30, or a person born with the Sun in the sixth house and no planets in the seventh will by the time they are an adult have developed the strong relationship requirements associated with the Sun in the seventh house. The sign that follows on from our Sun sign is therefore an extremely important one, whether it is occupied or not (very often it is, due to the close proximity of the planets Mercury and Venus). Karmically speaking this sign represents the stage of life towards which we are heading – more than likely our future Sun sign. Progressions and transits, plus any planets already situated in this sign help us to prepare for this future life by giving us a sample of the complex changes of characteristics which are required. It is vital, therefore, that we learn to understand and accept this progressed sign, in order to feel at ease during the next lifetime. We should not look back – planets in preceding signs to the Sun indicate lessons we have not learnt during the previous lifetime. This sign is also often highly represented in a birth chart, but it tends to produce more difficulty and obstructions in life.

MOON

By transit: This represents two and a half days of fleeting concern. Our daily moods are very much affected by the transiting position of the Moon. I have noticed that I am much more communicative when the Moon is going through Gemini, more lively when placed in Sagittarius, but somewhat tearful, tired or depressed when it slips into Pisces or the twelfth house. Those with the Moon prominent in their chart react much more noticeably to these swift transits. When the Moon returns to the phase it occupied at birth – New, Full, First Quarter and so on, one tends to feel uplifted or refreshed – a situation which could be regarded as a little rebirth.

By progression: Progressed Moon moves approximately one degree a month, thereby completing its twenty-eight-day cycle in approximately just under two and a half years. It is the most active of the progressed planets, but the least likely to cause major disturbances. It does, however, indicate two and a half years of restless, emotional disruption in the area occupied. It is not the easiest of progressed movements to control and can indicate a spell of unreasonable, childish behaviour when the subject is operating negatively. Its influence within a certain area is rarely permanent and it is surprising how quickly the subject is able to forget previous needs and desires when the Moon moves on to new territory. This is more apparent and easier for the subject to accept when the Moon is moving from an unoccupied house towards one that is natally occupied.

MERCURY

By transit: The transits of Mercury are rarely very consequential. Occasionally the planet remains stationary for about a week and during these times Mercury may be felt as a stronger influence. Generally speaking the planet enhances our communicative abilities in the area of life through which it is travelling. It is slightly more potent when transiting the mutable houses – third, sixth, ninth and twelfth and the mutable signs Gemini, Virgo, Sagittarius and Pisces, and particularly strong when occupying its own natal sign and house. It does not have much effect upon unoccupied houses, except to enliven them with added communication.

By progression: The progressions of Mercury are not so important as those of the Sun and Moon. Like the Sun, it remains in one sign or house for a great length of time. Major changes do occur when it changes sign or house – but these are purely on a mental level and are therefore usually less noticeable than most other progressions. The more prominent Mercury is within the chart, the more strongly the progressions will be felt as regards the communicative faculties – which may be increased or decreased according to the sign occupied. The house position can indicate new interests or learnings being engendered, especially when Mercury enters an otherwise unoccupied third or ninth house. The subject will automatically think a great deal about the affairs of the house in which progressed Mercury is placed.

VENUS

By transit: Venus transits usually last a little longer than those of Mercury – but only just. Providing the planet does not form any major difficult aspects during its swift transit it tends to bring harmony, peace and luck to the area occupied. Sometimes, however, it can also add laziness, materialism and sensuality to the character, especially when posited in the areas prone to such traits, such as the second house. Its frequent cycle (usually a year or less) ensures that the subject does not feel an overriding need to adjust when the planet enters an unoccupied house.

By progression: More important than the transit, but not so powerful as the progressions of Sun and Moon. Venus softens and feminizes everything it touches. A male's chart which is dominated by masculine forces, such as positive signs and the planets Mars, Jupiter, Sun and Uranus, is likely to benefit from a Venus progression into a passive sign, whereas a chart which is dominated by feminine placements, whether it belongs to a male or a female is likely to experience the transit of Venus into a passive sign or house as a further element of weakness. Venus projects charm and tranquillity but rarely strength of character. Therefore the progressions of Venus into an unoccupied sign, although immediately apparent and able to bring expansion (or restriction, if entering a less harmonious sign) of creative, aesthetic and materialistic values to the subject, rarely create momentous changes within the lifestyle.

MARS

By transit: The transits of Mars can be very important, especially when Mars experiences one of its intermittent (approximately once every two years) long spells in any one sign or house. The vibrant, powerful energy of Mars which is usually manifested on a physical level, is far more noticeable than the quiet, subtle energy of Venus. When Mars enters an unoccupied house it can appear that the subject has undergone some radical change. Suddenly, without apparent cause, the subject may throw himself feverishly into the activities represented by the house. Mars truly has the capacity to bring alive quiet, empty areas with full gusto – sometimes too much so, thus causing danger. Usually, however, the transits of Mars are swift – returning approximately once every two years. Most adults, therefore are able to adjust easily to these bursts of activity and find them helpful and stimulating. No other planet whilst transiting an unoccupied house can seem to effect so much minor but swift change.

By progression: Mars does not move quickly by progression. Any change of house or sign, therefore, is quite momentous. A person born with Mars in Pisces, is for instance, bound to feel highly energized and vigorously renewed when his progressed Mars slips into Aries. Although he will still retain his Mars in Pisces qualities, a new, more positive manner of approaching life will result. The change can be drastic – undiluted Mars energy can be extremely difficult to control when the relevant house or sign is natally unoccupied, and the subject may need much time to adjust. All transits or progressions into unoccupied houses tend to be more noticeable and often more difficult to handle, but none more so than progressed Mars with its raw, direct energy.

JUPITER

By transit: The yearly sojourns of Jupiter within one sign or house are quite important. Its twelve year cycle ensures that almost everybody experiences the benevolent, expansive qualities of this planet in their unoccupied houses several times throughout their lifetime. Sometimes Jupiter can bring apparent destruction or tragedy into our lives, but this negative reaction is more likely to occur when the house is occupied by one or more planets which have not been utilized positively by the subject. Usually, when entering an unoccupied house, all the natural benefits of Jupiter tend to arise, but once again it is up to us how we use these opportunities. If we abuse them or fail to acknowledge them this can generate negative Jupiter energies, even when the house or sign are natally unoccupied.

We all vitally need these transits of Jupiter through our empty houses – its yearly stay ensures that we have enough time to feel the effects and to adjust to the changes being wrought. The transits of the personal planets will rarely instigate a major event (although they may also be occurring at the same time as major transits), whereas the transits of Jupiter are able to do so. When Jupiter enters an empty seventh house, for instance, it presents the subject with a marvellous opportunity to form a permanent relationship and many marriages do occur at this time. Another example would be a person with no planets in the eleventh being allowed the opportunity to make friends and join in group activities. The enthusiasm for such activities is likely to wane somewhat when Jupiter moves into the twelfth house, but will rarely disappear completely. Unlike the transits of the personal planets and those of Uranus and Neptune, the transits of Jupiter seem to have a relatively permanent effect. Couples stay married after Jupiter has left the seventh house, and a subject remains involved in his new career when Jupiter moves from the tenth house into the eleventh house. This degree of permanency is undoubtedly one of the reasons why Jupiter is so expansive in its movements, and is therefore of particular benefit when moving through unoccupied houses.

By progression: Occasionally within a subject's lifetime, Jupiter will progress into a new house or sign, and thereby cause major changes in his life – but even when doing so its entry is slow – taking at least two or three years – and the effects may not be felt for quite some time after that, but providing it moves completely into the unoccupied area, the subject will slowly reap the benefits of this mighty planet's presence.

SATURN

By transit: Many people fear the transits of Saturn more than those of any other planet, yet it stays in one sign or house for less than half the time of Uranus and a fraction of the time of Neptune and Pluto, and its energies are far more controllable than those of the three outer planets. But Saturn is the planet that represents fear, restriction, limitation, burdens and responsibilities and it seems to be these facets of life which we dread, rather than the sudden disruption of Uranus, the escapism of Neptune, or the volcanic eruptions of Pluto. The humdrum dreariness of daily life so aptly represented by Saturn does not engender much pleasantness, charm or excitement. Yet Saturn can also teach us much, especially about our karmic obligations. Once we learn to accept Saturn's limitations with patience and fortitude, we can actually reap many benefits from its transiting presence.

Those with Saturn strongly placed in their chart find it more difficult to cope with Saturn transits. In my own chart Saturn is relatively weakly placed with very few aspects, and I have rarely found transiting Saturn to be a worrying or fearful influence, even when it forms difficult aspects. It does, in fact, seem to open up the areas it moves into with a helpfulness more indicative of a Jupiter transit, but I have yet to meet another person who continually experiences Saturn in this manner. The depth of despair which some people experience during major Saturn transits is, unfortunately, far too common a reaction.

Because the unoccupied signs and houses are so strongly affected by the entrance of a transiting planet, it is reasonable to suppose that the entrance of Saturn into one of these areas can be extremely frustrating. An area which heretofore has required little attention quickly becomes fraught with problems, setbacks, limitation and difficulties – mainly minor, but seemingly insurmountable at the time. The transits of Saturn truly test our patience, stamina, reliability and serious intentions. If we do not knuckle under to the new requirements of Saturn then it will enforce its persisting energies until hopefully we are able to understand.

When an area is already occupied by one or more planets, the life-patterns of that house are already being utilized to a greater or lesser degree. Saturn's entrance tends to control these patterns and make them more structured and useful, but upon entering an empty house Saturn has nothing to grasp, and must therefore begin its vigil from the very beginning. Providing the lessons of the house have been well-learned in previous lifetimes this should present no problem – it should not take long for the subject's unconscious mind to recall the conditions emphasized during past lives and work them successfully into his present life. If, however, the Saturn transit exposes future testing ground, great restriction and limitation can arise due to the subject being unable to handle the transit. The transits of Saturn are rarely forgotten – life is never quite the same even when Saturn passes into the next sign or house. Ideally, we should have learnt much about how to handle life in order not to make the same mistakes again.

By progression: Unless Saturn reaches the exact degrees and minutes of another planet, these progressions are too slow to be of any consequence. On the rare occasions that Saturn does enter a new sign or house, which is unoccupied it does, however, become a very significant progressed factor within the chart.

URANUS

By transit: Most people feel the transits of Uranus very acutely. Its action is dynamic and wholly disruptive, but not always detrimental. Sometimes a person needs to be 'pushed' into action or experience enforced change. The effects of Uranus upon an unoccupied house can be extremely difficult in the initial stages of entry, especially when moving into a fixed sign or house. The subject may assume that he has the affairs of the house (or sign) in question totally under lock and key and is in complete control, until Uranus rudely forces entry without any thought for the consequences. The subject must, however, be prepared to move with the times. Uranus demands immediate responses and action. If a natal planet occupies the relevant house or sign, the responses should, through familiarity, be easier, but when the area is unoccupied the response is far from automatic and the affairs of the house need a little more time to be explored and regenerated into the subject's lifestyle. But Uranus is remarkably impatient and does not allow time for adjustment. The transits of Uranus into unoccupied areas are therefore extreme and sudden tests of past karmic lessons which should have been resolved, or sharp, painful tests of future existences.

By progression: Uranus rarely moves more than two or three degrees during a lifetime, and is seldom used within progressions.

NEPTUNE

By transit: The transits of Neptune are often subtle and insidious in their action – often appearing to be of little significance on the surface, but tumultuous deep within. Therefore, Neptune's entry into an unoccupied house, might at first seem to have little effect. Changes are gradual and often centred around five words beginning with the letter 'd': disintegration, disorientation, dissolution, deception and disillusionment.

Neptune's main aim in life is to transcend or dissolve all boundaries and confinement. It is for this reason that when operating on a very positive level Neptune is capable of great spirituality, and remarkably inspired creative endeavours. Empty houses, however, have very little for Neptune to 'work on'. There is nothing to dissolve or uplift as there would be when one or more planets are placed in the house. Slowly, however, the effects of previous karma are brought into the light and explored. A person may find a hidden talent reveals itself when Neptune moves through an empty house, but they might also be called upon to relive and/or relearn a very distant karmic lesson. In my opinion Neptune and Pluto represent very 'old' karma, whereas Uranus and Saturn represent more recent karmic obligations – which causes their transits to be more acutely felt than those of Neptune and Pluto.

By progression: Due to its extremely slow movement, Neptune is rarely used within progressions.

PLUTO

By transit: Pluto and Neptune transits work in a similar manner, but the slow-heated undercurrents which eventually lead to Plutonian volcanic eruptions seem to render Pluto transits more traumatic and transformative, often involving some form of violence or aggression. In common with Neptune, Pluto's energy is slow to take effect in unoccupied houses, but once having gained a foothold, it is relentless in its actions. A subject who previously may have declared, in all honesty, that something (or somebody) was totally uninteresting could find the disinterest miraculously transformed into dedication or obsession. Pluto transits are very permanent. Death, birth and total transformation can occur even when it moves through an empty house – for instance, Pluto moving into an empty fourth or tenth house, can just as easily indicate the loss of one of the parents, as it does when forming major aspects to the Sun or Moon. When moving at its slowest, Pluto takes over thirty years to travel through one sign or house. Therefore, whatever area it is occupying must eventually become an integral part of the subject's character.

By progression: Due to its extremely slow movement, Pluto is rarely used in progressions.

2

Lack of Qualities

Active/Passive Polarity, Quadruplicities and Elements

Voids which occur in any of the above-mentioned groupings of qualities are highly meaningful in chart interpretation, especially when related to karmic obligations.
When assessing natal charts for voids, I do not take into
account the Angles, the Moon's Nodes, nor any other
calculated point in the chart. Nor do I consider the
planetoid Chiron. All the voids studied in Chapters 1
and 2 of this book embody a deficiency of planetary
energies within certain areas, commodities or qualities of
life. Although the inclusion of important features, such
as the Ascendant and Midheaven, should always be
taken into account when reviewing the 'whole' situation,
because they can, in many cases, reduce the effects of
voids, they should be regarded as sensitive points in
which the planetary energies are able to manifest more
powerfully, rather than focal outlets of pure energy. Only
the ten discovered planets of our solar system should
therefore be used when interpreting voids.

The sections which follow make frequent reference to
a sample of 400 charts studied from my files, mostly
from this century (approximately 10 per cent are prior to
this). Almost a quarter of these belong to famous – or
infamous – personalities. The remainder are those of
clients, friends and family. Though of course the results
might well be different if one were able to study large
numbers of charts for people born in other centuries, it

is hoped that the present study will serve to stimulate further enquiry.

POLARITY VOIDS

A total lack of either the Active (Positive) or Passive (Negative) polarity is somewhat rare. After all, it involves one half of the chart being untenanted. In my sample of 400 charts, almost a quarter of which belong to well-known personalities, only three possess a polarity void – a figure which is actually equivalent to less than one per cent of the population. It is not surprising, therefore that the few who do possess this striking void, are extremely unusual or unique individuals. Their birth charts contain at least six empty signs or houses, but the actual chart shaping is not usually of the Bundle type, but rather that of the Splay type – an individual who does not conform to any recognized lifestyle.

The total lack of one of the polarities does not, however, seem to engender extreme imbalance of character. It must be remembered that in these exceptional cases, two elements of the same polarity are missing, and the subject should theoretically be projecting either wholly negative or wholly positive characteristics. This, however, is rarely the case, for just as two negatives can become a positive, or as the see-saw having reached the bottom can only go up again, the person with a polarity void is able to transform the natural expression of his planetary placements: negative becomes positive and positive becomes negative. The situation can also be likened to the yin and yang lines of the *I Ching*, in which all the completely yin lines eventually change into yang lines, and all the completely yang lines transform into yin lines.

These total transformations can only occur with complete voids – such ratios as nine positive to one negative, or eight negative to two positive are extremely imbalanced and likely to cause great problems within the psyche of the subject. It is worth noting, however, that ratios of 5:5 or 6:4 are very beneficial as they signify balance, especially when the Ascendant and Midheaven equate with this balance. To my mind the optimum combination for today's pressurized mode of living is six positive to four negative.

When considering polarity voids, the subject should ideally, also possess the same quality of sign on his Ascendant and Midheaven, but unfortunately when taking these two points into consideration the perfect void becomes virtually extinct. Of the three examples from my files two have an opposite polarity Ascendant and one has both the Ascendant and Midheaven placed in the opposite polarity. All three cases struggle with the projection of their Ascendant, which is in total antipathy to the remainder of their chart and is therefore blocking them from being able to follow their powerful karmic path.

Most voids indicate karmic strength, but the subject with a polarity void does in reality possess at least three separate voids – the relevant active or passive polarity, plus two lacking elements – all of which supplement an above-average amount of empty houses. These subjects are almost undoubtedly very old souls who are gifted with an abundance of karmically inherited talent in areas of life which are normally of little concern to them (the empty houses.) They do, however, possess several extremely concentrated areas which demand careful and constant attention. The subject is rarely allowed to relax and must always guard against negative attitudes in these highly occupied areas. Despite their talents it is invariably an uphill battle for them to be able to express these gifts freely, especially when the Ascendant is all too often combative or destructive to their inner requirements. It is probably these few remarkable people who are the nearest to becoming ' perfect' souls, but this very fact decrees that in many respects their allotted paths are the most difficult of all to follow.

ACTIVE (POSITIVE) VOIDS – FIRE AND AIR

The subject has all ten planets placed in passive (negative) signs, indicating that through his many past lives, he has learnt the lessons of fire and air and is able to make free use of these qualities in his character if he so desires. But during his present lifetime the accent is on the passive signs and the areas of life in which they fall. These are the areas which require great concentration on his part – and the qualities of the active group are available to help him achieve these aims. A person with this void will rarely appear to be very lively, enthusiastic, or over-communicative. They need to be introspective, meditative and subjective in order to fulfil their karmic obligations. Although the qualities of the active polarity are readily available on an unconscious level, any abuse of these qualities – conscious or otherwise – would be extremely detrimental to the subject's karmic path. These people are quietly positive, determined and resourceful. If the element of water predominates, then they will also be compassionate and caring, but will need to watch their powerful emotional needs. If the element of earth predominates they will be highly astute and practically capable with a love of the earth, but should watch their tendency to be over-materialistic.

PASSIVE (NEGATIVE) VOIDS – WATER AND EARTH

The subject has learned most of the lessons of the passive quality during past lifetimes, and therefore does not need to be introspective, emotional or quiet within his present lifetime. These qualities, are, however, readily available to him, especially if he has a passive Ascendant to work through. Because the subject inwardly ' knows' all there is to know about the depths of the passive qualities, he is readily able to understand others, and is often highly intuitive, especially if he possesses a predominance of fire signs. He does not, however, suffer fools gladly – the intense concentration of the fire and air elements renders it difficult for him to curb his impatience and utilize his enthusiastic, communicative abilities shrewdly and carefully. Too much negative use of a powerful fire element could render the subject impulsive, reckless, crude or selfish. With a predominance of air signs the subject craves excessive mental stimulation, and is in danger of becoming dejected or depressed if these needs are not gratified.

QUADRUPLICITY VOIDS

After having checked through my 400 example charts, I was rather surprised to find that the number of quadruplicity voids was so low in comparison to the number of elemental voids, though of course one would expect some difference owing to the fact that a quadruplicity void involves having one-third of the chart untenanted, as opposed to only a quarter untenanted with an elemental void. In the case of the cardinal and fixed qualities, the percentage results were similar to those of the polarity voids. (Table 1).

Table 1: *Quadruplicity voids*

Cardinal Voids	Fixed Voids	Mutable Voids
3	3	8
(less than 1%)	(approx. 1%)	(approx. 2%)

One very interesting factor which emerged from this study, was the fact that although only 25 per cent of the example charts were those of famous or well-known personalities, two of the cardinal voids and one of the fixed voids belonged to this grouping. From the eight mutable voids, however, only one is from this group. It would appear, therefore, that mutable voids are twice as common as cardinal or fixed voids, especially amongst the general population, and that cardinal and fixed voids tend to enhance a subject's special unique brand of talent.

All three of the personalities involved in the cardinal and fixed voids are extremely well known, and would certainly appear not to be lacking in the quality represented by the void – in fact the reverse situation seems to apply. Bob Dylan and Mick Jagger have cardinal voids, Sean Connery a fixed void.

Most people would not argue that the qualities of self-assertiveness, enthusiasm and self-interest usually expressed by strongly cardinal people are very apparent in the characters of both Bob Dylan and Mick Jagger. Neither of them would have been able to achieve such prominence in their lives had they lacked the necessary drive and assertiveness inherent within the cardinal quality. Sean Connery possesses an aura which seems to ooze fixity and dedication. It would appear, therefore, that quadruplicity voids, although rare, are just as important as all other voids. They, too, represent talent and/or well-learned lessons brought forward from a previous lifetime. A person lacking in one of the quadruplicities automatically possesses an abundance of the qualities related to that grouping – all of which are accessible and readily integrated, albeit somewhat unconsciously, into their daily lives. They do not need to work at improving these qualities unless major transits or progressions activate the empty areas.

When one quadruplicity is lacking, however, the remaining two groupings become extremely important, with powerful lessons to be learnt within their relevant expression. Ideally, there should be a balance between these two groups, but often one grouping is emphasized and is therefore a problematical factor within the chart. Too much of any one quality is very difficult to control and the subject usually has many lessons to be learnt within the appropriate signs and houses.

CARDINAL VOIDS

There are only three of these in the sample. One might expect them to be more common in the charts of famous people than in the general population, since the qualities of self-absorption and the overriding desire to be first which are very prevalent within strongly cardinal people are not easy to control, and the lessons involved very difficult to learn. Indeed, of the three, two are from the Famous category which makes up 25 per cent of the total. Those few who achieve enlightenment on how to utilize the cardinal energy in a purely positive way have truly earned the right to be automatically placed in 'first' position, and be admired for their success. If the 'fixed' quality predominates, the subject can be stubborn, pig-headed, lacking in adaptability, obsessively habitual, oversexed and highly opinionated. If 'mutable' signs predominate, the subject is more easy-going and instantly likeable, but can be somewhat moody and lacking in tenacity or determination.

FIXED VOIDS

A total lack of fixity or 'staying power' can initially seem disastrous, but upon noting the enormous endurance portrayed by Sean Connery it must be realized that a void in this quality can endow the subject with a natural gift for sticking at something to the very end. These people have learned in their past lives that in order to achieve anything worthwhile they must carry on regardless. If a predominance of cardinal signs supports the lack of fixity, the subject is able to reach the heights of his profession, but they must guard against selfish attitudes, over-enthusiasm and vanity. With a predominantly mutable support, the subject can be highly restless and indecisive, but adaptable, malleable and able to see all sides of a situation.

MUTABLE VOIDS

Although a certain amount of mutability is desirable within any birth chart, too much is often regarded as a sign of weakness or lack of strength. By general standards, it would appear that individuals who are strongly cardinal or fixed, or who possess voids in these areas, are usually more prominent or successful in life than a person who has the mutable quality emphasized by planetary activity or voids. My example charts seem to validate this, as the eight who possess this void do not appear to be as strong or effective as the six cardinal and fixed individuals.

Seven of the eight mutable void examples are members of the general public, the eighth being the young Princess Eugenie, daughter of Prince Andrew and Sarah Fergusson, who at the time of writing is too young to be assessed for her lack of mutability. Within all mutable void people is an innate ability to adapt or move with the times, but it is not very apparent to the casual observer, especially when the fixed quadruplicity is dominating the chart. Mutability is in itself somewhat intangible or dualistic in nature like the signs it represents (Gemini, Virgo, Sagittarius and Pisces) and is better utilized as a complement to the cardinal and fixed qualities, rather than as a strength in its own right.

People with many mutable signs in their chart, or those with a mutable void, possess talents which operate better when empowered by another person, although the talents inherent within the mutable void subject are more easily assimilated into the natural expression of character. Mutable void people are often magnetic, but difficult to understand – a factor which is probably due to the strong influence of cardinal and fixed qualities. When cardinal signs predominate, the subject is strong, lively and helpful in nature, but also self-seeking and lacking in observation concerning the innermost needs of other. Fixed signs predominating render the subject more wilful, determined and set in his ways. If fixed signs far outweigh the cardinal, then the subject is liable to experience great trauma in life, often caused by negative, obsessive habits.

ELEMENTAL VOIDS

These voids are reasonably common. My sample of 400 charts revealed 79 elemental voids, distributed as shown in Table 2.

Table 2: *Distribution of elemental voids*		Table 3: *No. of years 1900–90 when at least one outer planet in element*	
No Fire	5	Fire	65
No Earth	36	Earth	41
No Air	25	Air	50
No Water	13	Water	71
	79		

This figure represents almost 20 per cent of the population and is surprisingly high when considering the dearth of quadruplicity voids. The extreme imbalance of representation can be partly explained by the distribution of the outer planets.

Table 3 gives, for each element, the total number of years 1900–90 when there was at least one outer planet in that element. On the basis of this table, one would expect there to be more fire voids than water, but in fact there are more than twice as many water as fire.

It was also fascinating to discover that elemental voids are almost twice as common as grand trines, which were 44 in number compared to the above figure of 79. Grand trines can be viewed as a similar but preliminary phase of elemental voids. The energy projected by these fortunate configurations is positive (but not always assertive) and cognisant, in contrast to the more subtle esoteric qualities of the voids. Grand trines used wisely become the voids of future lives.

When breaking down the number of grand trines and elemental voids into subsections of male and female charts and famous and non-famous personalities more interesting factors arose (Table 4).

Table 4: *Sexual and Famous/Non-famous distribution of grand trines and elemental voids*

	Grand Trines				Element Voids		
	Total	Male	Female		Total	Male	Female
Fire	17	13	4	Fire	5	2	3
Earth	8	5	3	Earth	36	14	22
Air	8	2	6	Air	25	11	14
Water	11	1	10	Water	13	4	9
Famous		Non-famous		Famous		Non-famous	
7		37		11		69	

(Distribution of the 400 charts = 25 per cent famous, 75 per cent non-famous)

When comparing the overall figures, it is interesting to note that the polarity elements of fire and water are higher in grand trines than they are in voids, whereas the opposite applies when looking at earth and air. In the male/female examples, although the ratio of female charts in the study was higher, the males figured more prominently in the fire and earth grand trines and were not very far behind with the fire voids. Overall, air emerged as the most balanced of the elements and both water grand trines and water voids more common with the female gender. Therefore, most of the resulting combinations seem to support the ideals of fire and air being masculine and active, and water and earth being feminine and passive.

With regard to the famous and non-famous personalities, neither grouping in the famous personality section quite reached the expected 25 per cent although the ratio of voids was slightly lower in comparison to the ratio of grand trines, thereby indicating that there is some evidence to support the fact that overt grand trines are more conducive to public success than the hidden attributes of elemental voids.

Within general interpretation a subject who is lacking in one of the four elements is supposedly unable or unwilling to express the quality associated with the relevant element, and certainly in some cases this appears to be true – Adolf Hitler lacked water in his chart and was seemingly unable to relate on an emotional level, although he was a very emotive orator. Vincent Van Gogh lacked the element of air and was renowned for his awkward and difficult manner of communicating. In other instances, however, this appears far from the truth – Margaret Thatcher is lacking in earth, yet there is much practicality, common sense and dogmatism in her character. Likewise Chris Evert, one of the most tenacious, stable tennis players of the 1980s, is also lacking in earth.

It has been suggested by many astrologers that some people, when lacking in a certain element, will contrive to compensate for their lack by expressing the qualities of the relevant element to excess. Personally I do not hold to this theory, as when viewed from the general interpretative level of relating the planetary energies to their positions within the signs and houses, it would be extremely difficult for anybody to express a quality which was supposedly absent from their chart. An abundance of planets in the houses relating to the missing element would help the subject to project the necessary energy but in a less direct manner. From a karmic viewpoint, however, the contradictory factors surrounding the circumstances of elemental voids have at their disposal the qualities projected by the missing element. It is easy to see how some of these people will be unaware that they possess these qualities – so deeply are the characteristics embedded into their unconscious, whilst others – probably those who are more tuned in to their inner psyches – will recognize the innate talents of the element and utilize them within their lifestyle – some successfully, and others – those who become greedy and choose to ignore their planetary karmic needs in favour of the inherited gifts – less successfully.

On a conscious level, all voids are difficult to integrate as part of the character. It is only when we allow the subtle, unconscious energy to flow automatically that we are able to benefit from the knowledge and talents ingrained within us from our past lives. It is vital that we never abuse the power of voids, as it is highly likely in so doing much previously acquired wisdom and learning is lost or damaged, which in our future lives will need to be relearned. Voids are there to support us when in need, not to prop us up throughout our physical lifetime. The high occurrence of elemental voids in birth charts, indicates that they represent an initial stage of karmic achievement and there are many people struggling to attain a higher karmic existence through such voids.

FIRE VOIDS

My example figures indicate that fire voids are the least common of the four categories. It is generally assumed that this void conveys a lack of drive, initiative and enthusiasm, or in some cases, due to over-compensation, an excess of these qualities. None of my five examples seems to project an obvious lack or compensatory factor. The one famous personality amongst these five examples is Ronald Reagan – a man whose fire qualities are kept under control and only utilized when absolutely necessary. This lack has not inhibited Mr Reagan in any way from success in several avenues of life – in fact the inner strength conveyed by a fire void has undoubtedly helped him to feel confident within himself. A famous example from outside the survey is D. H. Lawrence.

Fire void people are rarely highly exuberant – unless they are abusing the element – but they are quietly magnetic, assertive and enterprising. They are usually more self-assured and outwardly balanced when air is the predominant element. A strong emphasis on water or earth with a little air is highly imbalanced towards the Passive polarity and could therefore cause feelings of insecurity, shyness and emotional dependency.

EARTH VOIDS

This is by far the most commonly represented group within my 400 examples but even taking into account extraneous factors one would still expect a similar out-

D. H. LAWRENCE

(Born on 11.9.1885 at 9.45 a.m. in Nottinghamshire, England)

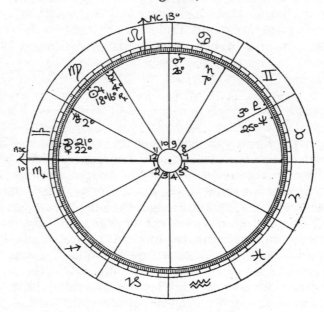

VOID DATA
Number of unoccupied houses – 7
Number of aspects – 13.   No quincunxes or oppositions
Jupiter only conjuct Sun

No fire

CHART 1.   *D. H. Lawrence*

come when using a larger survey figure. Why is this so? Why should earth voids predominate so significantly? Perhaps it is because earth is usually the element which most of us feel closer to – it is physical, material and concrete whereas the other three elements, especially fire and air are far more abstract in character. We are surrounded throughout our lives by physical components of the earth element – buildings, land, structure, money, possessions – and of course the very essence of earth itself – nature. Regardless of whether we possess planets in earth signs or not, every day of our lives we are made aware of the significance of the earth element. The lessons of earth must therefore be easier to learn, but conversely the hardest of all to maintain. Earth void people have at their disposal the means to ensure a stable, secure financial outlook. They are naturally in tune with the earth, but unless operating on a positive level they may deny, reject or abuse these innermost needs. The element of earth is very easy to abuse – we do it all the time via pollution and wholesale destruction of the earth's natural resources.

It was therefore not surprising to discover that most of the thirty-six earth void examples within my files do project, in some form, a materialistic outlook on life. Several of the examples are wealthy or financially secure people with little need to worry about their station in life – but they do. Over half of the examples are members of the general public who work with money, land or structure, or who are closely associated with these facets of life. The ability with which they are able to use their voids successfully and positively in their lives is indicated by the varying levels of competency in handling financial and material matters. The truly learned earth void subject does not allow greed for material and physical resources to enter his life, because if he does so, he is abusing his karmic gifts and talents. Money and material success flow automatically towards earth void people, providing they are prepared to give way and let go of their earthly instincts. On the other hand, these people must always be aware of the rewards that a positive attitude towards materialism will bring. As always, it is a fine dividing line between balance – which is the ultimate aim of life, or imbalance which eventually results in destruction or loss. Margaret Thatcher and Chris Evert – neither of whom possess a particularly easy chart – seem to have utilized their earth void energy quite successfully to date, whereas Marilyn Monroe and Mozart, who also possessed earth voids appear to have struggled throughout their lives to achieve this fine balance.

AIR VOIDS

I was somewhat surprised to discover that air voids were the second highest in quantity after earth. From a purely physical viewpoint I would have expected them to be lower, as air is the most intangible and difficult to contain of all the elements. It is constantly surrounding us and we cannot live without it, yet it is invisible and uncontrollable, whereas fire, earth and water can all be seen, and controlled if necessary. The lack of physical substance within the air element must surely render it less comprehensible than the other elements and thereby more difficult to understand and conquer on a karmic level. Yet it would appear that more people have grasped the intricacies of air than they have the subtleties of fire and water.

Traditionally, the air element void represents a lack of being able to communicate with ease on a mental level and/or difficulty in putting ideas across. Certainly, some air void people do seem to find these facets of life difficult – several of the twenty-five examples in my files verify this theory. But also amongst these examples is the chart of Prince Andrew – a man to whom communication seems to present few problems, and the charts of several writers or authors. Writing is one of the main avenues of communication and one would not normally expect a person with a lack of air to be able to co-ordinate his ideas clearly on paper.

As with all other voids, but particularly with the elemental voids, contradictions occur. Voids are no easier to analyse or categorize than signs and houses with planets placed therein. Extremes in negative and positive characterizations are likely to occur in both situations. In all instances, however, the level of positivity achieved seems to depend upon the accumulation and control of karmic knowledge. Those who have earned voids in air would appear to have mastered something very special – the mind. But in today's technical, materially based world it is easy to allow matter to rule the mind, and therefore very difficult for an air void person to sustain his karmic obligations. Air talents should be used wisely and sparingly in conjunction with the faculties provided by the prominent element placements within the chart. If fire predominates over water and earth, the subject is more able to project himself in a communicative sense – especially if the sign of Sagittarius is strong within the chart. If earth or water are stronger, however, the subject may find himself entrenched in materialism or swamped by emotions that are difficult for him to express.

WATER VOIDS

In the same manner that fire is completely active/positive in action with all three signs of the element being ruled by masculine planets (Mars, Sun and Jupiter) water is essentially passive/negative in action with all three signs being ruled by feminine planets (Moon, Pluto and Neptune). Water is a polarity to fire just as the Sun is to the Moon, yin to yang, black to white, and so on. The remaining two elements of air and earth do not form this clearly defined polarity of masculine and feminine – both elements possess a sign which has the androgynous Mercury as a ruling planet, and the highly feminine planet Venus further complicates matters by its rulership over the masculine sign of Libra. It is interesting to note, therefore, that voids in the elements of fire and water are much lower than voids in air and earth. Could it be that the lessons of complete objectivity (fire) and complete subjectivity (water) are the hardest of all to learn, and when taking into account the initial phase of voids as represented by grand trines, that generally it is the male of the species who succeeds more quickly with the lessons of the fire element and the female who succeeds more quickly with the lessons of the water element. Males with water voids and females with fire voids, therefore are very unique people with very special and highly intense karmic obligations to meet in life. These are the people who might seem to have a total lack of either fire or water, but inwardly possess such tremendous capacity to utilize the missing element. Adolf Hitler was one such person. The lack of water in his chart is often held responsible for his many atrocities and apparent inability to maintain a warm, loving relationship. On the surface it seems that Hitler totally submerged his water void, instead of using his special gifts of intuition and compassion in conjunction with his planetary placements. He was obviously very frightened of showing the extreme feminine psyche within himself, and abused the void by pretending it did not exist.

In complete contrast another water void abuse occurred when one of the four males from my examples chose to live his life as a woman. He was unable to dispense and use wisely the feminine attributes rendered from a previous lifetime. This man is extremely psychic and intelligent and is undoubtedly a very old soul, but the misuse of his water void will surely demand recompense in a future existence. If a water void person is strong in fire placements, then an imbalance exists which requires extremely fine attunement. Water void subjects are easily brought to tears and often appear to be extremely sensitive individuals. They are often mistaken for being born under a water sign. When this occurs it is an indication that the subject is not handling his water void talents in a wise or positive manner.

3

Unaspected Planets

Over the last decade I have come to the conclusion that far from being inconsequential components of astrological interpretation as some astrologers would lead us to believe, unaspected planets are extremely important and should always be analysed with care and reverence within all spheres of astrological analysis, but especially so within natal charts.

WHAT CONSTITUTES AN UNASPECTED PLANET?

Strictly speaking, a wholly unaspected planet does not exist, for if one were to take into account all the many minor aspects which can be used in astrology, unaspected planets would become virtually extinct. It is my opinion, however, that most of the minor aspects are too insignificant to be of any value in interpretation, and although the merits of such aspects as the semi-square and quintile are worthy of closer examination, the use of too many minor aspects only serves to cloud and confuse the issue of interpretation.

All astrologers utilize the four major aspects which have proven to be of significance, namely the conjunction, square, trine and opposition. Most astrologers incorporate the sextile, and many, like myself, add the remaining two aspects which are divisible by 30 degrees

– the semi-sextile and the quincunx. These seven aspects form the backbone of aspect interpretation, and throughout this chapter (unless mentioned otherwise) a planet is only regarded as unaspected if it does not form any one of these aspects. Some astrologers have decided to dispense with the semi-sextile and quincunx when assessing unaspected planets. This certainly raises the percentage of unaspected planets considerably, but I view the trend as somewhat hasty because I believe that both of these aspects are relevant within interpretation – the quincunx being of particular significance. My own chart contains no less than five very tightly orbed quincunxes which appear to work on a subtle, but powerful level. It is, however, worth noting any planet which forms only one minor aspect to another planet, as this becomes an 'almost unaspected' planet and as such is a very common occurrence. The minor aspect is heightened in its effect and should be treated more like a square or trine, but the energy flow of the planet is also strengthened and can be almost as influential as a completely unaspected planet.

As with the Qualities, one should disregard the Angles and Part of Fortune, along with all other calculated mathematical points, when assessing whether or not a planet is unaspected, as these points do not emit physical energies and are therefore unable to influence the unaspected planet to any great degree. Obviously, an unaspected planet situated at one of these points is likely to appear more prominent within the characteristics of the subject, but this is due to the angularity and open position of the planet rather than a mutual flow of energy between the two factors.

The degrees of orb allowable for any aspects are always debatable, but I usually adhere to the same rules which I apply to any calculated birth chart – 8 degrees for a conjunction, square, trine or opposition, 4 degrees for a sextile and two degrees for a semi-sextile or quincunx.

THE SIGNIFICANCE OF UNASPECTED PLANETS

An unaspected planet represents pure, unmitigated energy within the sign and area in which it is placed. It is not hampered or challenged by difficult aspects such as squares and oppositions, nor softened or rendered more harmonious by easy aspects such as trines and sextiles. An unaspected planet cannot become part of any major planetary configuration such as a grand trine or a t-square. It is invincible and stands alone in a birth chart, emanating power and glory. Its energy can be likened to that of an animal who is allowed to roam and eat freely without any human interference or aid. At times the animal might struggle for existence but in doing so, he learns how to fend for himself, and is able to live his life in the manner that nature intended. A study of unaspected planets allows us to observe how the true energy of each planet manifests itself within our characters.

Karmically speaking, unaspected planets are a gift from a past life – a life (or many lives) in which the lessons relating to the particular planet have been learned and integrated positively into the personality. As with all karmic situations related to voids in the birth chart, however, it is very easy to abuse or relate negatively to an unaspected planet. The subject discovers that he has a surfeit of pure energy at his disposal which, in order to fulfil his present karma, he must use wisely – but without the help of the other planets he may find it very difficult to channel the energy in a positive manner. Hence the discrepancy between two people with the same unaspected planet – one of whom is using and controlling the energy wisely and is successful in life, while the other allows the energy to run wild and spill everywhere.

Unaspected planets represent very strong karmic testing ground and are usually associated with very old souls. They represent the last stage of the karmic journey – the unoccupied houses being the first stage. But it is very easy to slip backwards on the karmic path, and a person who abuses the wonderful gift of an unaspected planet may find that a future life will once again involve difficult aspects to that planet, with more lessons to learn and obstacles to overcome.

Unaspected planets are nearly always overtly expressed in the characteristics of a person. The energy of the relevant planet streams forth in abundance (regardless of the sign and house it occupies) and very often dominates the entire character. It is easy, for instance, to mistake a person with an unaspected Mercury for a Gemini, even when they possess no planets in this sign. Before studying unaspected planets I was sometimes puzzled and disappointed to find that although a certain sign or planetary influence was radiating powerfully in the individual's aura, upon erecting the birth chart there appeared to be a complete absence of the specific influence, but my study of unaspected planets opened up new vistas in interpretation.

The person whom I had immediately recognized as strongly Scorpionic or Plutonian, but who had no planets in Scorpio or the eighth house, and a weakly placed Pluto, actually possessed an unaspected Pluto. The child whom I looked after for several years, whose appearance and behaviour were typically Piscean/Neptunian, but who was in fact a strong Leo, with no water in his chart, possessed an unaspected Neptune. My own son, who was inadvertently the instigator of my studies into unaspected planets, projected the pure qualities of an unaspected Moon – nurturing, compassion and finely tuned sensitivity – from a very early age. The sign of Capricorn, in which the Moon is placed (on the ascendant) seemed to take a back-seat and both his personality and appearance are far more typical of a lunar type person than a Capricornian, although, unfortunately as he has grown older, in accordance with the demands made upon him by society and schooling, the caring qualities have been pushed somewhat into the background in favour of the more serious, cautious qualities of Capricorn. I was gratified to find these and many more instances of correlative facts about the characters of those born with unaspected planets, all of which greatly helped to authenticate my studies and beliefs in the issue.

Unaspected planets are not common. From my sample study group of 400 charts there were only 65 examples with such a void, which represent an approximate 17 per cent of the population distributed as shown in Table 5.

Table 5: *Charts with at least one unaspected planet*

Sun	13	Jupiter	7
Moon	7	Saturn	5
Mercury	10	Uranus	4
Venus	6	Neptune	5
Mars	5	Pluto	3

The low percentage achieved by the three outer planets is generally explainable by their slow-moving cycles and the long-standing aspects which they have formed with each other this century. For instance the sextile between Pluto and Neptune which began in the early 1940s will, apart from a few breaks (when using a 4 degree orb) continue well into the 1990s. The sextile is a relatively mild aspect which, when occurring between these two planets, is completely generational and, unless forming part of a major planetary configuration such as a yod, should be analysed quite succinctly within chart interpretation. When disregarding this aspect the number of unaspected planets involving these two planets rises quite sharply, easily equalling or even exceeding the figures of the personal planets. On no account, however, should any major aspect between two of the three outer planets be disregarded. For instance, the powerful conjunction between the planets Uranus and Pluto in the sign of Virgo which occurred during the middle to late 1960s has proved to be devastating in its effect.

The sixty-five charts with unaspected planets were also divided into Famous and Non-famous categories, as in the previous section. (Remember that 25 per cent of charts studied were of famous people.) The result was Famous, 15; Non-famous, 50. These figures correlate very well to the expected 25 per cent, but when the Famous category is further classified into the ten planetary groupings, some unexpected results occurred. (See Table 6.)

Table 6: *Number of famous individuals with unaspected planets.*

	Famous	Total		Famous	Total
Sun	6	13	Jupiter	2	7
Moon	1	7	Saturn	2	5
Mercury	1	10	Uranus	0	4
Venus	0	6	Neptune	2	5
Mars	1	5	Pluto	0	3

The unaspected Sun figures reach almost 50 per cent, which far exceeds the expected 25 per cent, but of the remaining nine planets only Jupiter, Saturn and Neptune have attained the 25 per cent target. It is well worth noting that the remaining personal planets – Moon, Mercury, Venus and Mars fare very badly in their contribution of unaspected planets in the charts of famous or notorious individuals. Perhaps this is to be expected when one considers the planets Moon and Venus, which are essentially, soft, passive planets, or when considering Mercury, which tends to be amorphous and prefers to take its shape from other planets, but it is somewhat surprising to see the exceptionally low overall figures for Mars, with only one-fifth being represented by famous people.

In all the attained percentage categories – Sun, Jupiter, Saturn and Neptune, the famous people involved are nearly all extremely well-known household names – four being prominent members of the present royal family. In these cases, it can certainly be said that unaspected planets are capable of bestowing wealth, genius, luck and an abundance of talent – which if used incorrectly can cause extreme negative influences, and is the case with the Yorkshire Ripper Peter Sutcliffe who, apart from the almost obligatory Pluto sextile Neptune, possesses an otherwise unaspected Pluto.

Surprisingly, it is not rare by any means for a person to possess two or even three unaspected planets. Seven of the sixty-five examples listed do actually possess two unaspected planets, the three famous examples amongst these being Prince Edward (unaspected Jupiter and Saturn), King Louis XIV (unaspected Sun and Neptune) and President John F. Kennedy (unaspected Sun and apart from Pluto/Neptune sextile, unaspected Pluto).

HOW UNASPECTED PLANETS WORK WITHIN THE CHART

UNASPECTED SUN

Each planet projects its own unique energy, and it would be somewhat presumptuous to say that any one planet is able to react better than another when unaspected, but it does appear from the sample charts that an unaspected Sun, apart from being twice as common as most of the other planets, does auger well for extreme fame and fortune. The Sun is undoubtedly one of the most important significators in astrological interpretation. When it forms difficult aspects, many problems need to be surmounted by the individual in order for him to feel useful and fulfilled within life. The energy of an unaspected Sun, however, is brilliant and dazzling. There is no better example of its magnificent projection than in the personality and popularity of King Louis XIV of France who was nicknamed 'The Sun King'. His actual Sun was placed in the sign of Virgo, 9 degrees away from the Midheaven, but it was not the characteristics of Virgo which dominated his life, but the powerful, unimpeded energy of the Sun. As if it were not enough, he also possessed an unaspected Neptune which was placed almost exactly on his Ascendant in the magnetic sign of Scorpio, and a virtually unaspected Uranus (one weak sextile to Mars). With such unusually strong planetary placements, it is very easy to understand why Louis was destined to become an extremely famous king.

People born with an unaspected Sun are rarely insignificant in character or quiet in nature – if they appear

LOUIS XIV

(Born on 5.9.1638 at 11.11 a.m. in St Germain-en-Laye, France)

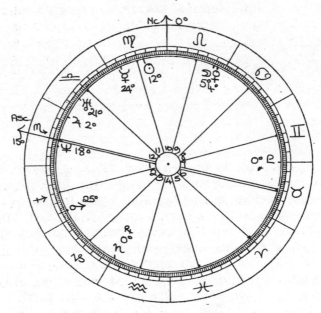

VOID DATA
Number of unoccupied houses – 4
Number of aspects – 11.   No semi-sextiles
Unaspected Sun, unaspected Neptune, almost
unaspected Uranus

CHART 2.   *Louis XIV*

to be so this is entirely due to other planetary placements. They possess a healthy ego, which can manifest in the growing child as noisiness, self-centredness and bossiness. This child really knows how to make his presence felt in any household, even if his sun is placed in one of the quieter earth or water signs, but as he grows older he usually learns how to control these powerful qualities. Occasionally, however, an obnoxious unaspected Sun child grows into an even more obnoxious adult, as is the case with Vincent Van Gogh, who found it difficult to channel his unaspected Sun in a chart which strongly represented all the various kinds of astrological voids, as well as some very challenging conjunctions. Most people with unaspected Suns, however, are popular, or well-loved individuals. Some, like Louis XIV, John F. Kennedy and Cliff Richard have succeeded in creating a massive projection of adulation. These are people who will never be forgotten. Even Van Gogh was idolized throughout his life by his brother Theo, who was always able to see the Sun shining through Vincent's strange personality, and it is no coincidence that many of his paintings seem to portray an image of sun-like qualities. He, too, will always be remembered.

But the most well-known unaspected Sun person of this era is undoubtedly our present monarch, Queen Elizabeth II, whose Sun is situated in the sign of Taurus in the fourth house – not a very open position or outgoing sign, but still very obvious to the general public, and undoubtedly even more so to the immediate members of the royal family. But it is very appropriate that the Queen is not the only member of her family to possess an unaspected planet, and that most of those whose planets are all aspected possess either very easily aspected charts or charts with very few aspects. All these facts seem to verify the theory that to be born into royalty is a status earned by an accumulation of previous incarnations in which many lessons of life have been assimilated. Most members of the royal family are very old souls, who have been given a life of ease in many respects but with many duties and responsibilities to perform.

Those born with an unaspected Sun have truly been

VINCENT VAN GOGH

(Born on 30.3.1853 at 11.00 a.m. in Groot-Zundert, Holland)

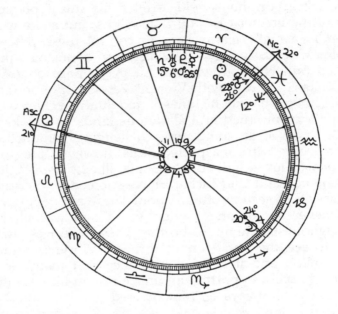

VOID DATA

Number of unoccupied houses – 7/8

Number of aspects – 15.　No quincunxes or oppositions
　　　　　　　　　　　　Saturn and Uranus only one
　　　　　　　　　　　　aspect each

Unaspected Sun
No air

CHART 3.　*Vincent Van Gogh*

honoured, and are usually vital, powerful and constitutionally strong individuals who know their worth, but
they must beware of ego-inflation and domineering attitudes.

UNASPECTED MOON

Despite the fact that a prominent Moon in a birth chart
often indicates success and public recognition, especially
when placed in the tenth house (note that Margaret Thatcher has the Moon placed in her tenth), when unaspected the Moon appears to become softer, more feminized and ultra-vulnerable, thus hindering the type of fame
often meted out to those with an unaspected Sun. Even
in the 1990s the attributes of kindness, compassion and
spirituality associated with a positive Moon are not so
readily accepted as the more dominant, masculine attributes of the Sun. After studying the seven example
charts in my files it became reasonably obvious that
people born with an unaspected Moon do not find life
particularly easy. They are soft, gentle souls struggling
to exist in a hard, material world. Theoretically, it should
be easier for a female to cope with an unaspected Moon,
but in reality it does not appear so – they are just as
prone to 'putting on' a brave face as are the males with
this placement.

The only famous personality amongst the seven listed,
is that of the famous scientist Louis Pasteur, whose chart
was littered with voids of all kinds – seven empty
houses, an active/passive ratio of 1:9, a void in the fire
element, a lack of opposition aspects, and of course the
unaspected Moon. This was placed in his eighth house
in the sign of Gemini (the only positive sign planetary
placement in his chart), well hidden from the public eye
– unlike his six planets in Capricorn, which were placed
in the open third house. Louis' chart is very spiritual
and extremely complex, and only those who knew him
well would have been bestowed with the honour of
seeing his intuitive, yet analytical unaspected Moon in
action. He was undoubtedly a very deep thinker (Moon

in the eighth, plus the accumulation of planets in the sign of Capricorn) who should have been able to rationalize (Gemini) his feelings and emotions in a very abstract manner.

It would appear that those with Capricorn or one of the other earth signs prominent in the chart, are more able to stabilize themselves and cope with an ultra-sensitive unaspected Moon. In fact all the seven examples from the study possess charts that are abundant in earth factors, either by possessing at least three planets in earth signs, strong second, sixth or tenth house placements, and/or an earth sign rising. Four of the charts possess extremely strong earth configurations, such as Louis Pasteur's, so it would appear that in order to survive in this technological, materialistic world, most unaspected Moon subjects are endowed with the practicality of earth.

Unaspected Moon people look sensitive and are easily mistaken for water sign subjects. Their eyes possess a sparkling, tearful or wistful expression and despite their outer demeanour which can at times appear confident and positive, upon closer reflection one is usually able to notice that their general expression is sad. Males with an unaspected Moon are usually very feminine or effeminate in appearance, and may seem physically weak, but they are stronger than they appear – the buffer given by the earth signs allowing them to build upon their constitution, especially as they grow older. As children, however, they often suffer from health complaints and various weaknesses, especially to the stomach and breast areas, which are ruled by the Moon. Both sexes are extremely attached to the mother, but there is rarely an antagonistic effect, such as is often experienced by those with a difficultly aspected Moon. The mother is usually highly sensitive, psychic and spiritually aware – in fact four of the seven examples possess mothers who are involved in healing or psychic work. I myself, as a mother of a son with an unaspected Moon, am included in this example.

These people feel a vital need to be wanted and appreciated, yet they find relationships difficult. The free-flowing positive energy of the unaspected Moon demands that they be givers in life, rather than takers, but sometimes they feel as if they are battling against a huge brick wall, for it is not always easy to be constantly giving out in a world that is full of 'takers'.

UNASPECTED MERCURY

When referring to the 400 sample charts, the number of examples exhibiting an unaspected Mercury is high in comparison to the figures for the remaining planets. In fact the combined figures for the two most commonly represented unaspected planets – Sun and Mercury – contribute more than one-third of the overall figure of sixty-five unaspected planets. This fact is somewhat surprising as these two astral bodies are never more than 28 degrees apart and often form a conjunction with one another. Even more frequently they tend to occupy the same sign or house, with Mercury living in the shadow of the Sun, and endeavouring to emulate the Sun's brilliance. It is very surprising, therefore, to discover an apparent lack of famous or even infamous subjects with an unaspected Mercury. I certainly would have expected this communicative planet, when unaspected, to be prominent within the charts of well-known celebrities – if purely from the point of view that this Mercury is able to talk itself into or out of any situation. But the facts seem to indicate that unaspected Mercury, in contrast to its close companion – the Sun – is far less likely to achieve fame or fortune than a Mercury which forms challenging aspects.

Mercury thrives when it is stimulated by other planets. Its androgynous character finds it difficult to settle or to relate for any length of time when there is no steadying anchor. When unaspected, and placed in a different sign or house to the Sun, the planet is out on a limb – an essentially weak planet with little form or shape, propelled into a role of prominence and individuality within the birth chart. When placed in the same sign or house as the Sun the problems are not so acute but still difficult for the subject to integrate into his lifestyle.

People born with an unaspected Mercury are restless, lively, intelligent individuals, who find it somewhat difficult to express themselves on a permanent, stable level. They possess oodles of talent, have many interests in life and can converse on almost any subject. They can be highly serious and intense, or quick-witted and fun-loving with a good sense of humour. Sometimes the same individual can express all these qualities in great abundance within an extremely short space of time. The everchanging Mecurial temperament operates on a consistent wave of peaks and troughs – the highest of summits being attained remarkably quickly, thereby effecting an equally swift and often hazardous decline. Unaspected Mercury does not seem to possess the tenacity, dedication or enthusiasm to stay on the bandwagon of success – there is a continuous underlying urge to move on, move out, give up or change direction. These people are forever searching for an anchor which is not personally available to them, but can sometimes be achieved through another person. This may be the reason why many unaspected Mercury subjects seem to marry or bind themselves to very stable or earth-orientated people.

The volatile, changeable nature of Mercury is never very easy to label or control even when aspected, but when unaspected (especially if placed in a mutable sign) the magician-like qualities of the planet render it almost impossible for another person to comprehend or decipher its divergent actions. Mercury is capable of performing many tricks – some very innocent and childlike, others remarkably devious. Mercury can be here one day, gone the next. The vivid imagination of Mercury is further accentuated when the planet is unaspected, and although this attribute can help with the many creative and artistic talents which the subject possesses, it can also help to highlight such negative traits as deception, lying, unreliability and instability. Generally, however, unaspected Mercury is capable of great charm, and this gift, allied to a thirst for knowledge and an inherently devious mind, usually ensures that this is a person who is well-liked and whose misdeeds are easily forgiven. Unaspected Mercury is a 'fun' person to be with and is often the 'life and soul' of the party.

UNASPECTED VENUS

A total of six people from 400 – a meagre 1½ per cent of the population is, I think, a very disappointing result for unaspected Venus, especially when considering that this includes no famous or notorious subjects. But in common with its feminine comrade, the Moon, unaspected Venus is essentially passive. It is also peace-loving, sensuous and somewhat lazy – often preferring to sit back and wait for the good things in life to fall into its lap. Without the strength of a closely aspected planet to help activate it, Venus tends to lose its identity within ideals of love, beauty and peace. Sometimes, however, the earthy, sensual side of Venus becomes rampant, leading to an unhealthy obsession with material wealth, possessions and/or sexual activity. When handled positively, unaspected Venus possesses a natural homing instinct for financial security, and one would expect to find many unaspected Venus subjects who are married, related or attached in some way to famous or wealthy people, their affluence and security thus being ensured.

My six examples are, however, ordinary citizens with nothing to set them apart from the crowd, save their attractive appearances, polite natures and well-respected characters. They do not possess the immediate likeable impact of the unaspected Mercury person, and can upon first meeting appear to be shy, diffident or unfriendly, but eventually their genuine love of humanity shines through. They can be either extremely generous or extremely stringent – much depends upon whether the positive or negative influences of the planet predominate.

As with all unaspected planets, the house position seems to be more important than the sign position. Unaspected Venus projects strong Venusian qualities regardless of the sign it occupies, but is usually more prominent in an 'open' house (first, third, fifth, seventh, ninth or eleventh). Venus is a very sociable planet and those with an unaspected Venus enjoy social occasions, but it would appear that without a planet to which it can harness itself, Venus, in common with its closest stellar body, Mercury, has difficulty in being able to project itself at its very best. At least three of my six examples are known to have led restricted or problematical lives as regards relationships. The bounteous assets which an unaspected Venus confers – abundant love and affection, a desire for harmony and an appreciation of beauty – are not easily recognized or readily incorporated into the subject's life. But Venus dreams about a perfect relationship and is invariably disappointed when love is not reciprocated in the idyllic manner created in her mind. Unaspected Venus is usually expected to be the 'giver' rather than the 'taker', but unlike it's feminine compatriot the Moon, Venus is rarely happy with an imbalanced situation, and can therefore be prone to consoling her wounds in the arms of another lover. Venus is, however, essentially loyal and does not enjoy being unfaithful, but the unquenchable thirst for love which is deeply ingrained within the planet's psyche far outweighs any guilt which may be experienced.

It is unfortunate that unaspected Venus does not usually possess the potential fame of an unaspected Sun, or the good fortune of an unaspected Jupiter, but it does endow its owners with a charm which is very rare in this technological, materialistic age.

UNASPECTED MARS

It was surprising to discover that in my sample of 400 charts there were less than half as many charts containing an unaspected Mars as there were charts with an unaspected Mercury or unaspected Sun. But in view of the massive reserves of energy (mostly uncontrolled) which an unaspected Mars is capable of engendering it is perhaps just as well that the overall figures are very low!

Mars can manifest its energy on many different levels.

When reacting positively a powerful Mars produces great athletes and sportsmen and/or courageous individuals who exhibit much determination and single-mindedness, but when being utilized on a negative level it encourages individuals to become warriors, warmongers, criminals, aggressors or libertines.

Mars is a difficult planet to control – even more so than Uranus, which at least possesses the advantage of ruling a fixed sign and is subsequently capable of a strange uniformity within its unusual behaviour patterns. Mars does not recognize boundaries – it rules the impulsive, self-centred sign of Aries, and therefore tends to leap into action without any forethought. Aspects to Mars can heighten or lessen its overall effect – an aspect from Saturn, for instance, will limit and control the enthusiasm and energy of Mars, for better or worse (depending upon the aspect). An aspect from Jupiter will expand the energy and render Mars highly excitable, over-optimistic and more likely to take chances in life. When unaspected, however, Mars can only be expressed through the house and sign it occupies. Its energy becomes pure, vital and rampant, with an urgent desire to move continuously forward. It is surprising, therefore, that there are apparently few famous or infamous subjects with an unaspected Mars. My study is far from conclusive, however, and includes very few politicians, athletes or criminals – all those whom one might expect to possess an unaspected Mars.

The only famous personality amongst my five examples is that of the actor Rock Hudson, who died from the sexually transmitted disease of Aids. His Mars was placed in the sign of Scorpio (no surprises here), in the second house, along with Saturn and the Sun, but it did not conjunct either of them or make aspects to any other planet. Mr Hudson would appear to have abused his unaspected Mars by projecting its formidable energy into his sexual life – although its placement in the second house also augered extremely well for his financial resources and earning capacity. The second house, however, is also the seat – or the beginning – of one's sexual libido. I always regard it as ruling raw, instinctual desires, which bear no relation to the refinement of sexuality based upon love and emotion as represented by the opposite eighth house. Rock Hudson's lifestyle was dominated by his second house Scorpio planets, especially the unaspected Mars, and one of the main factors responsible for his death would appear to have been a sad case of unaspected Mars lacking control and direction.

Another case from my study is that of an unfortunate girl who has led an extremely unstable life. She cannot control the violent outbursts which have led her to a life of petty crime, drug addiction, and prison sentences. She is a confessed lesbian, and is HIV positive. Her unaspected Mars is placed in the sign of Pisces – a sign which finds it difficult to contain the fiery energy of Mars. Her reactions are based upon emotion, feeling and instinct. She also possesses a void in the air element, but unfortunately it would appear that her inherent ability to communicate in the easy, logical manner associated with this void has not been utilized – a fact which is probably at least partially due to the dominant force of her unaspected Mars.

There is no doubt in my mind that unaspected Mars is usually far too powerful for most people to control and is therefore capable of taking over a person's identity. When observing those who appear to be normal, healthy individuals, as is the case with my remaining three examples, there is an obvious underlying strength and power which appears to be ready to erupt at any time. Unaspected Mars does not dither between one factor and another – it knows its own mind, and can be devastatingly cruel, hard or vindictive.

One of these three subjects possesses an unaspected Mars in the first house in the sign of Scorpio. This person is extremely hard towards herself – she drives relentlessly on, disregarding her own physical and emotional requirements and ignoring all warnings concerning her health, body and appearance. She is self-centred about herself in a most reckless, determined manner, and her likes and dislikes which are highly intense are readily projected into the personality. She is the type of person one cannot ignore, but I feel that eventually the unaspected Mars, although abundant in determination when placed in Scorpio, will prove to be her downfall if she does not endeavour to come to terms with its all-consuming energy.

Unaspected Mars seems to possess a reckless, self-destructive quality which is highly inflammable – an energy which vitally needs to be harnessed into a worthwhile strenuous activity such as sport, otherwise the energy is directed inwards towards the physical body which is gradually destroyed in the process.

UNASPECTED JUPITER

The magnanimous, expansive qualities of Jupiter seem to fare better than the brash energy of Mars when unaspected. As one might expect, an unaspected Jupiter adds optimism, buoyancy and luck to any birth chart. In common with the Moon, it appears that many of the problems usually associated with difficult Jupiter aspects disappear completely when the planet does not form aspects. Until recent years Jupiter was always regarded as the 'great benefic'. Ancient astrologers believed that Jupiter could do no wrong and that when strongly placed in a birth chart it was almost certain to bestow riches, luck and happiness. Nowadays, astrologers tend to believe that Jupiter, like other planets, can manifest both positively and negatively. Unaspected Jupiter, however, does appear to reap more rewards than it does problems. It acts as a buffer against any difficulties in the birth chart. In several of my examples, despite possessing somewhat difficult charts, with many challenging aspects and in two cases a very prominent Saturnian influence, the unaspected Jupiter still manages to shine optimistically through. These people can put on a brave face and smile through any adversity. They can shrug their shoulders and allow the planetary energies to flow, because deep within them is instilled the confidence and innate wisdom of a powerful Jupiter. There is always something very likeable about these people, even when the Ascendant and remaining planetary positions decree otherwise. They often possess a good sense of humour, a keen sense of justice and a generally benign attitude towards other people. In keeping with the size of the planet, when unaspected, Jupiter can add much girth, height or general structure to an individual's frame.

Jupiter, as one might expect, also fares better than Mars (and Moon, Mercury and Venus) when it comes to the famous category of personalities. Two out of a total of seven examples is not as high as I would have expected, but one prominent member of the royal family – Prince Edward – does have this regal planet unaspected in his seventh house – a position which augers well for an advantageous marriage or business partnership. Jupiter is one of the planets (the other being Neptune) which is associated with the theatre and acting, and certainly Prince Edward has projected his unaspected Jupiter into a love of the stage.

Another famous personality who possessed this planet, unaspected in the sign of Cancer in the fifth house, was Janis Joplin, the deceased American blues singer who rose to fame during the 1960s. Janis' Jupiter was always in evidence in her character, which was highly sensitive and emotional (typically Cancerian), and was one of the major factors for her extreme popularity and rise to fame. She did, however, also possess an almost unaspected Mars in the somewhat adventurous, unstable sign of Sagittarius. The one very weak aspect it formed – a trine to Neptune – did not really help to anchor the profound energy of her Mars – and in the end it appears that she was unable to control her reckless Mars in favour of the more fortunate Jupiter, and her accidental death from a drug overdose was the fatal result. The fact that she is well-remembered is not only due to her talent, which was no more remarkable than hundreds of others of her era, but to her unaspected Jupiter, which had the ability to put her on a pedestal and make her the 'queen' of rock.

An unaspected Jupiter should be regarded as a welcome feature in any birth chart as it bestows luck and fortuitous opportunities, but it is up to the subject to

decide whether he is 'big' enough to grab these opportunities.

UNASPECTED SATURN

Mention the planet Saturn and one is immediately con-
fronted with groans and complaints from most individuals who understand astrology. Saturn must surely
be the most maligned planet within our solar system.
The blame for everything in life that we suffer most from
is usually laid at this large planet's stolid feet. Yet an
unaspected Saturn does not bring disaster and gloom –
merely a responsible, kindly and well-trusted nature.
Some planets seem to operate better when unaspected
than others and Saturn is one of these. When unaffected
or lacking in influence from other planets, Saturn is able
to manifest its energy on a more smooth, uninterrupted
and fearless wavelength. Certainly, these individuals are
serious conformists who are deeply aware of their duties
in life and may at times feel weighed down by them,
but their Saturnian energy seems more in keeping with
the positive characteristics of the sign of Capricorn than
the negative insecurity factors which often plague this
sign and its ruling planet.

Two immediate members of the royal family possess
an unaspected Saturn – these being Prince Edward, who
also possesses the contrasting unaspected Jupiter, and
the young Prince Henry. Both these princes tend to live
in the shadow of their respective brothers, and appear
to be quiet, respectable citizens. One expects, however,
that at some time in their lives, their unaspected Saturns
may demand that they carry burdens and responsibilities
which will far outweigh their personal needs in life.
Prince Henry especially, who does not possess the buffer
of an unaspected Jupiter, and who has Capricorn rising,
with a strong twelfth house, is likely to feel his unaspected Saturn most powerfully as he grows older.

Although an unaspected Saturn by itself seems to operate surprisingly well, if there are other placements within
the chart which signify that the subject needs space and

freedom, then the unaspected Saturn will be at odds with this need, for instance, one of my examples also possesses an unaspected Neptune which is very strongly placed in his birth chart. His desire for all the Neptunian facets of life does tend to override the unaspected Saturn, but he then becomes beset by guilt, worry and the responsibilities of a full family life. He finds it extremely difficult to cope with these two unaspected planets which are both pulling at divergent angles. As a result he is often ill, and seemingly unable to cope with life on a practical level.

People with an unaspected Saturn are rarely popular, and are often difficult to approach or understand, but they are immensely trustworthy, honourable and reliable.

UNASPECTED URANUS

It is difficult to find a completely unaspected Uranus, Neptune or Pluto in my sample. Yet, if one of these three outer planets is unaspected then the owners of such a planet usually have much to offer society in the way of individuality and talent. Unfortunately, however, it is difficult to control an outer planet and for every person who utilizes one of these unaspected planets successfully in life there is another who becomes prey to their negative influences and either collapses under the pressure or becomes infamous rather than famous.

If one discounts minor aspects between the three outer planets (not those that occur between the outer planets and the personal planets), namely, the semi-sextile, quincunx and sextile, a situation arises whereby the planet(s) can almost be regarded as unaspected. I note this condition on birth chart forms as 'virtually unaspected'. When such planets are included in the overall calculations for unaspected planets the figures rise very sharply to encompass approximately 25 per cent of the population. After having studied unaspected planets for a considerable time I am inclined to interpret an outer planet as unaspected even when it does form a minor aspect with another outer planet, as the effects of such an aspect seem to manifest purely on a very broad generational level – note the examples stated previously for Peter Sutcliffe (a Pluto aggressor) and John F. Kennedy (a Pluto victim), both of whom possess(ed) a virtually unaspected Pluto.

It is a strange (Uranian!) fact, however, that even a virtually unaspected Uranus is far less common than a virtually unaspected Neptune or Pluto. It is even more surprising that not one of my 25 per cent of famous personalities possessed an unaspected or virtually unaspected Uranus – the closest example is that of Louis XIV's Uranus, which only formed a weak sextile to Mars.

Two of my four examples are children, who do seem to exhibit some claim towards extreme individuality – one of them being a musical prodigy who exhibited some extremely rebellious traits in his pre-school years. Unfortunately the remaining two are female clients to whom I gave postal readings, and I am therefore unable to judge the authenticity of their unaspected planets. It does seem, however, that in addition to being rare, unaspected Uranus does not manifest in such a galvanistic, outgoing or excitable manner as one would expect. Uranus is the higher octave of the planet Mercury and it would be reasonable to assume therefore that the planet is more active when involved in aspects with other planets. An unaspected Uranus, although gifted and quietly unique, does not seem to stand out in the crowd in the same manner as a highly aspected or angular Uranus. When unaspected the excitable, disruptive energy of Uranus is far less effective, and therefore more able to be expressed positively. The child musical prodigy mentioned above lost his rebellious, aggressive attitudes when his Uranian talents were fully utilized. From the small amount of examples I have to judge, it would appear that pure Uranian energy is androgynous, easier to channel and relatively harmless when compared with the energy manifested by a highly aspected Uranus.

UNASPECTED NEPTUNE

A completely unaspected Neptune is rare in my sample – approximately one in eighty people, but the instances of virtually unaspected Neptunes are much more frequent, and the majority of people who possess such a Neptune exhibit characteristics and qualities very indicative of Neptune's changeable influence. No other planet is capable of such diversity of expression as Neptune. When utilized positively the infinite beauty, spiritual wisdom, aesthetic ideals and wonderful inspiration of the planet shine through. Negative expression, however, leads to degradation caused by drugs, sex, alcohol or extreme weakness of character. There are also many shades of expression falling between the highest and the lowest attunement, and in many cases a strongly Neptunian person can project characteristics which manifest on many different Neptunian levels.

But although those born with an unaspected (or virtually unaspected) Neptune do vary in their projections, none of the examples in my files have fallen to the lower levels of Neptunian expression. It certainly appears that those with Neptune angular and/or difficultly aspected are more likely to suffer the extreme highs and lows of the planet.

A person with an unaspected Neptune is likely to possess some inspirational gift, usually of an artistic nature – such as music, dance, drama, art, healing or psychic ability. Despite the fact that they can be shy, inhibited and lacking in verbal communication skills, they usually possess a fascinating, highly magnetic aura which draws others towards them. They are highly adept at catching people in their fine but strong nets, then letting them go when they have served their purpose. They are also very good at escaping or vanishing into thin air when the going gets tough, then reappearing when matters have settled down.

Unaspected Neptune does not have to face the challenges of major aspects – its energy is therefore clearer and purer. These people may appear to live in a dream world of their own, but they know exactly where they are heading in life (albeit intuitively) and what they want to do. All the examples in my files appear to be surprisingly strong characters in many respects, although most of them have struggled through a strange childhood in which they were either showered with too much love or deprived of emotional support.

Louis XIV's unaspected Neptune certainly helped him become a legendary monarch, and miraculously escape from the difficulties which were rife during his era. He seemed to have the knack of disassociating himself from anything nasty or underhand, even if he was guilty of such action.

Another famous personality with a virtually unaspected Neptune (only a semi-sextile to Pluto) is Frank Sinatra. The fame achieved through his singing and acting career is certainly a Neptunian influence, but the unaspected element of the planet appears to have helped him (and others) to utilize it in a more stable manner. Many extremely famous personalities in the music and drama field have prominent (angular or highly aspected) Neptunes in their birth charts, but the negative influence of Neptune eventually takes its toll as it did in the case of Elvis Presley and Marilyn Monroe – two remarkably talented highly Neptunian individuals who allowed the negativity of Neptunian addiction to filter through into their lives.

Unaspected Neptune is stronger, and more centred and therefore less likely to fall prey to the extreme negative influence of the planet.

UNASPECTED PLUTO

Anybody who possesses this planet unaspected – or virtually unaspected – is likely to project abundant Plutonian qualities. The pure unharnessed energy of Pluto is so powerful that it can easily become dangerous to its owner, as is the case with John F. Kennedy. His virtually unaspected Pluto helped to give him power and control over his country but also attracted the ultimate violence inflicted upon him through his untimely death, thereby causing him to become a Pluto victim. Patty Hearst (virtually unaspected Pluto) the American heiress, who was kidnapped by terrorist revolutionaries in February 1974 and coerced into helping them in their raids, also, for a while, became a Pluto victim.

There is no doubt that Pluto attracts violence, eruptions, death and aggression when operating negatively. Even a positively projected Pluto tends to emit an undercurrent of suppressed anger or intense emotion. All Plutonian people enjoy power and control, especially when the planet is angularly placed or highly aspected. But in common with its comrades Neptune and Uranus, when completely unaspected the negative influence of Pluto appears to be weakened. My three examples of pure unaspected Pluto are all ordinary individuals who possess the innate Plutonian quietness of character, intensity of emotion and strength of purpose, but not one of them shows outwardly obsessive or aggressive qualities. It appears that the pure energy of Pluto is therefore powerful and strong, but not naturally destructive, as often appears to be the case when Pluto forms difficult aspects. Those with virtually unaspected Pluto, however, do not seem to be quite so balanced and very often fall prey to the negative influences of Pluto.

Pluto is generally regarded as ruling the whole of the life-process – birth, death and rebirth. It also rules the deeper constituents of sexuality (the lighter elements being ruled by Mars). An interesting chart which emphasizes these features of Plutonian energy is that of Marie Stopes (unaspected Pluto). Marie was a pioneer in birth control and author of books on sex education. With two planets (Mercury and Venus) in the sign of Scorpio and two planets in the eighth house (Saturn and Neptune) Marie's unaspected Pluto was in unison with much of her chart and thus enabled her to utilize the powerful energy in an extremely positive manner.

Others with virtually unaspected Pluto do not fare so well. Peter Sutcliffe, the Yorkshire Ripper (Ascendant unknown), possesses such a Pluto which he utilized on an extremely violent and obsessive level. One feels that he had the power to use his Pluto in a highly positive

MARIE STOPES

(Born on 19.10.1880 at 4.10 a.m. in Edinburgh, Scotland)

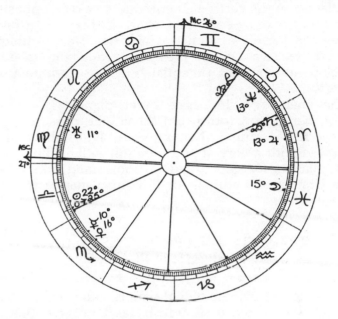

VOID DATA
Number of unoccupied houses – 5
Number of aspects – 15.   No squares
Unaspected Pluto
No planets in physical degrees. No angular planets

CHART 4.   *Marie Stopes*

manner – his chart being very strong in voids – a Bundle type shaping with eight empty houses (planets only situated in the four signs Gemini, Cancer, Leo and Libra), no planets in the earth element, and a void in opposition and quincunx aspects. His chart is that of a highly developed karmic existence which has been completely abused. He was given the power and the talent to develop his spiritual potential but chose not to use it correctly.

The energy of the three outer planets is, without doubt, harder to control, but those who possess a pure unaspected Uranus, Neptune or Pluto have been endowed with a very special rare gift – the ability to use these planets for good, and to understand how a truly pure Uranian, Neptunian or Plutonian manifests.

TRANSITS AND PROGRESSIONS TO UNASPECTED PLANETS

All unaspected planets will at various times form aspects through the medium of transits and progressions. All those who possess unaspected planets will therefore experience the difference in energy when the planet(s) forms challenging or benign aspects.

A planet which is not usually hindered or helped by aspects will generally find it difficult to adapt to long-lasting major aspects. A person with an unaspected planet is an individualist who is used to operating alone within the respective planetary energy and tends to reject or resent even the kindest of interferences such as trines or sextiles. Hard aspects such as squares and oppositions may prove to be very damaging to the unaspected planet's mode of action. These are true karmic tests of the highest and most difficult calibre. It is during aspects of these kinds that a person with an unaspected planet will tend to become confused and project the negative energy of the planet.

I have recently observed the effects of Saturn, Neptune and Uranus all traversing over my son's unaspected

Moon in Capricorn (on the Ascendant). Although no catastrophic changes have taken place – he is young and children are much more capable of resisting the negativity manifested through difficult aspects – I have noticed that the more caring qualities of the unaspected Moon have been subjected to a few powerful inner battles. I have seen him struggling with himself (the personality), his conscience and his need to be protective and nurturing, and his desire to change and become more male-orientated. The influence of Neptune has created a chaotic and disorderly streak, whilst the effect of Uranus has forced him to be more rebellious and detached from his family. I doubt whether his unaspected Moon will ever be quite the same, but I am hoping that with Uranus moving further away from his Moon he will finally regain much of his previous sensitivity and caring. Any such buffeting upon an unaspected planet must take its toll, but a truly highly developed soul should be able to weather the storm.

Trines and sextiles give added benefits to the unaspected planet(s), but very often the subject does not know how to accept the help being offered and the chances will therefore slip through his fingers.

People with unaspected planets are usually battlers. They are aware from a very early age that they are different or unique. Sometimes they would rather be one of the crowd and will make attempts to fall into line with the masses, without much success. When aspects occur to challenge the unaspected planet's single-minded energy, the subject may feel even more out on a limb as he endeavours to understand the changes erupting within his character, but the sooner he realizes that he is a 'special' person and is ready to utilize his powerful energy positively then he will quickly advance into the realms of highly developed spiritual karma.

4

Aspect Lacks

Aspects form an extremely important and highly complex part of astrological interpretation, their significance being paramount in the final intricate analysis of a birth chart. It takes years of study and observation to come to a full understanding of the expression of each aspect, especially the less intrusive, subtle influence of the minor aspects. A full cognizance of the efficacy of aspects cannot be achieved until many individual birth charts with the same aspects are carefully studied. Two people with the same aspect can react very differently to its energy. For instance, a person with Mars square Jupiter who has the signs Aries and Sagittarius prominently placed in his natal chart, will react more strongly to the aspect than the person who possesses no planets in these signs, but he should also be more attuned to the aspect and therefore more able to cope with its powerful influence.

I should at this point make it clear that all the references to aspects (or lack of them) here and throughout the book relate purely to the seven most commonly used aspects, namely the conjunction, square, trine, opposition, sextile, semi-sextile and quincunx. For the first four I use an 8 degree orb, for the sextile one of 4 degrees, and for the last two one of 2 degrees.

It is an unfortunate fact that most of the aspects traditionally labelled as 'malign' – the square, opposition, quinqunx and often the conjunction – are difficult to control and utilize positively and therefore tend to generate problems and challenges in people's lives. Conversely, the effects of the supposedly 'benign' aspects, namely the trine, sextile, semi-sextile and sometimes the conjunction, although beneficial and harmonious, are easily submerged and neglected, especially when there are many malign aspects in contention. Benign aspects, do, however, seem to give protection from the traumas experienced through the hard aspects.

OVERALL QUANTITY OF ASPECTS

All aspects, be they major or minor, modify the flow of pure planetary energy. Hard aspects can cause the energies to become blocked, restricted, frustrated or angry, whilst soft aspects can debilitate the energies, thereby causing lack of response, passiveness and apathy. Any aspect is capable of creating complex and often antagonistic reactions within the subject's psyche. It is therefore reasonable to assume that the less aspects, especially the hard aspects, that are formed in any birth chart, the less challenges, traumas and difficulties the subject will be liable to experience. It is a fallacy that charts with few aspects indicate a weak character. Generally, the reverse applies. A potentially strong chart contains as many voids as possible, and after years of study, I have observed that a lack of aspects is usually associated with well-developed individuals, who often appear to be old or wise souls. The fewer aspects there are in a birth chart, the fewer lessons there are to learn within the present lifetime. Much of this theory is supported by the fact that many extremely famous people who have led (or who are leading) seemingly charmed, or easy lives, possess fewer than the average number of aspects in their charts.

When assessing whether the number of aspects in a birth chart is high, low or average, I do not include the aspects formed by the Ascendant or Midheaven. These are not planetary energies and aspects from planets to these points do not normally react in the same manner as those occurring between planets. The following hypothesis is suggested as a means of helping to verify the difference between planetary aspects and aspects to mathematical points.

Two cats, representing the pure, cosmic energy of Mars and Uranus, meet unexpectedly whilst on the prowl. Both are living creatures, with their own unique personalities, but both also see themselves as leaders of their species and possess a common urge to conquer one another. If they united their energies a powerful conjunction would be formed, which although fraught with difficulties could actually work quite well. The reaction between these two cats, however, is to protect their individual supremacy, and they begin to fight, thereby forming a square or opposition aspect. A long battle ensues with one cat eventually emerging the victor. On his way home, the same cat comes across an unexpected obstacle – the cat flap through which he normally enters his home is stuck. The flap is an inanimate man-made object which can be likened to the Ascendant, Midheaven, or any other mathematically based point within a birth chart. No matter how much energy the cat produces to fight this obstacle, the flap will not fight back or produce energy of its own accord, though it may eventually become unstuck if the cat is lucky enough, or clever enough to solve the problem. It is an entirely different matter to meeting another cat.

The total number of aspects which can theoretically be formed between planets in any one birth chart amounts to forty-five, but it is uncommon for more than thirty to be present and extremely rare for a subject to possess in excess of thirty-four (none at all within my 400 example charts). Most people's aspect ratio falls somewhere within, or very close to, the average figure of fifteen to nineteen aspects. Twenty-one or more aspects should be considered as being above average, and fourteen or less aspects as below average. The chart with the highest number of aspects in my sample belongs to a child born in April 1989. She possesses thirty aspects, comprised purely of conjunctions, sextiles, squares and quincunxes,

JOSEPH HUNTLEY
(Grandson of Author)

(Born on 3.12.1987 at 8.45 a.m. in Croydon, England)

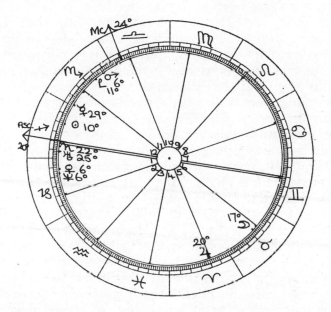

VOID DATA
Number of unoccupied houses – 8
Number of aspects – 9.   No squares or quincunxes
Unaspected Mercury.   Sun and Moon only one aspect each
No air

CHART 5. *Joseph Huntley (Grandson of Author)*

but one planet – Jupiter – is virtually unaspected. Needless to say, this is a very complex chart. The placing for the lowest number of aspects is shared between my own grandson, who was born in December 1987, and Prince Henry, who was born in September 1984, both of whom possess only nine aspects. It is interesting that these three contrasting, and unusual ratios all belong to children born in the 1980s, and therefore several more years must elapse before one is able to observe and judge the effects of their birth charts.

Many members of the royal family possess charts that are low in aspects. The Queen, Prince Charles, Princess Anne and Prince Edward are all examples, and Prince Andrew's chart, although slightly higher in aspects, is very benign. Princess Margaret and Princess Diana, however, possess more challenging birth charts. Several other extremely famous household names whose charts are low in aspects are – Cliff Richard and Adolf Hitler (ten aspects each), and Louis XIV (yet again!) and Albert Einstein (eleven aspects each). The overall proportion of famous personalities who possess charts which are relatively low in aspects is high – again propounding the theory that skills and talents are more able to flourish in a chart that is allowed to flow more freely and does not possess too many obstacles in the form of aspects. Difficult aspects in a birth chart which is already low in voids indicates a deeply indebted karma with many lessons to be learnt in life. If there are many hard aspects in a chart which is otherwise plentiful in voids, the subject is probably having to pay the penalty for a previous existence (most recent) which was not fulfilled in the manner intended by the laws of karma.

TYPES OF ASPECT VOID

A chart low in aspects does not necessarily indicate a charmed life even though the potential for success is higher than average. A chart with ten aspects which are all squares, oppositions or quincunxes is going to be more difficult to understand and work with than a highly aspected chart mainly represented by trines and sextiles. Generally, however, the lower the amount of aspects, the more likelihood there is of a particular aspect void existing. But it does not always follow suit – the previously mentioned child who was born with thirty aspects possesses three aspect voids – the semi-sextile, trine and opposition. This is very uncommon, however, and I would expect that as she grows older the child will discover that she has very specific, repeated messages of learning in life which are related to a highly unusual karma. Prince Henry with his nine aspects also possesses three aspect voids – semi-sextile, opposition and quincunx. Cliff Richard has voids in the semi-sextile, square and quincunx, and my young grandson has two aspect voids – the square and quincunx. Note that the three aspects generally thought to be the most challenging – the square, quincunx and opposition – are strongly represented as voids within the abovementioned examples.

Each chart in my sample was checked for lack of aspects. Table 7 shows the results.

Table 7: *Aspect voids*

Aspect Void	Total No. from 400	Approx % population
No conjunction	15	4%
No squares	16	4%
No sextiles	18	4.50%
No trines	18	4.50%
No semi-sextiles	110	27.50%
No oppositions	118	29.50%
No quincunxes	150	37.50%

The degree of orb used for this study adhered to my usual format – 8 degrees for the conjunction, square, trine and opposition, 4 degrees for the sextile and 2 degrees for the semi-sextile and quincunx. It is not surprising, therefore, that the figures for aspect voids in the conjunction, square and trine are far less than for the semi-sextile and quincunx. The figures for the sextile and opposition, however, are unexpectedly out of proportion, there being too few sextile voids and far too many opposition voids. The lengthy sextile which occurred between Neptune and Pluto in the 1960s and 1970s must account for the low figures in sextile voids, and to a certain extent the high figures for opposition voids would seemingly be due to the fact that throughout the latter part of this century the individual orbits of the three outer planets have gradually been drawing closer together. It is still surprising, however, that such a major aspect as an opposition should be very high in voids. When aligning the general absence of aspects to karmic development, it would appear, therefore, that after eliminating the minor aspects – quincunx and semi-sextile – the elimination of the opposition is the next step for a developing soul's karma. If this theory is correct, however, then the sextile is more important than is generally now thought to be the case.

The four major aspect voids were further divided into the Famous and Non-famous categories, as shown in Table 8.

Table 8: *Aspect voids divided into Famous and Non-famous categories*

	Famous (25% of 400)	Non-famous (75% of 400)
No conjunctions	3	12
No squares	4	12
No trines	3	15
No oppositions	28	90

The ratio for the lack of squares in famous personalities – one-third of the overall figure – is higher than the target of one-quarter – a fact which supports the hypothesis that a void in squares helps to achieve success and balance within the life. The conjunction voids are in perfect ratio to the total number of subjects, but the opposition voids in the 'Famous' category fall just short of the targeted 25 per cent and the trine voids for this quarter of the population are also well below the expected ratio, illustrating once again that the placement of trine aspects in a birth chart is usually a helpful factor in life.

Many very famous personalities do, however, possess challenging aspects in their birth charts, but after much study of the general representation of aspects and aspect voids, I have come to the conclusion that those subjects who possess many hard aspects, especially those formed by the outer planets to the personal planets, always seem to suffer more trauma, heartache, obstacles and challenges in life when compared to those people whose charts are low in hard aspects. Fame and success can be attributable to many different factors and those with hard aspects often exhibit strength and determination of character, but they also have many crosses to bear, due to a 'ragged' or confused karma in which they have abused some of the gifts earned in previous lifetimes. People whose charts are low in aspects but high in aspect voids and benign aspects are often born into a life of ease, and the few who are not so fortunate are more able to achieve harmony or success as they mature into adulthood.

The close movement of the four outermost planets during the 1980s has heralded the birth of many children who possess unusual birth charts, which are high in voids of all kinds. These include: more unoccupied houses and Bundle type shapings (all planets grouped tightly together in a space of 120 degrees), and a spate of voids in the element of air, partly due to the placement of Saturn, Uranus, Neptune and Pluto in passive signs during the latter half of the 1980s – which has also produced more voids in the active/positive polarity. The occurrence of two or more unaspected planets in one birth chart is also more prevalent, and, due to the close-knit composition of many of these birth charts, this generation has also produced a very high number of voids in quincunx and opposition aspects. All of which is quite impressive and indicates that many children of the 1980s are 'old souls', who are being reborn for a specific purpose in life. As we go into the 1990s, this trend will gradually decrease. It will be the early part of the twenty-first century when the exceptional 1980s children will be maturing into adulthood, and hopefully enlightening us as to why they are here.

SEMI-SEXTILE AND QUINCUNX VOIDS

These two aspects are considered to be minor by most astrologers, although the quincunx has been gaining in the popularity stakes and is now considered by some to be a fairly major aspect with its influence being mildly challenging, difficult or stressful with a predisposition towards health problems. I personally (my chart has several quincunxes) have rarely found this to be so and consider that the subtle influence of this aspect needs far more research. It is interesting to note that the semi-sextile is the only aspect which does not form part of one of the four major planetary configurations (grand cross, grand trine, T-square and yod) which gives support to the classification of this aspect as the least influential of the seven.

Quincunxes represent the highest overall number of voids – nearly 40 per cent of the population do not possess one, whilst the number of semi-sextile voids is 10 per cent lower. The fact that a quincunx is the most commonly eliminated aspect does suggest that karmically it could be considered the weakest of the seven aspects and representative of the easier karmic lessons in life. A few astrologers see the semi-sextile and quincunx as being similar in influence and energy, but more charts contain semi-sextiles than they do quincunxes. I have noticed that certain charts are predisposed towards quincunxes, tending to contain three or more, whereas semi-sextiles are often solitary aspects. Both aspects involve completely contrasting elements, but the relative closeness of the planets involved in a semi-sextile suggests that it is an easier aspect to understand and utilise on a positive level. Generally speaking, therefore, it may be marginally beneficial to possess a void in quincunxes rather than semi-sextiles.

All aspects are capable of bestowing talent and ability, but the three lesser aspects (sextile, semi-sextile and quincunx) and the trine give more accessible, karmically inherited talent. With the quincunx, however, the expression of this talent is rarely easy, especially before middle age. Voids in quincunxes (providing there is not a surfeit of squares and oppositions) enable a subject to express his natural talents freely. Voids in semi-sextiles (especially when many hard aspects are present) can cause blockages in expression and less opportunities for advancement.

SEXTILE VOIDS

Sextile aspects do not seem to fall into any category and are therefore somewhat unique – their 4 degree orb being higher than the minor aspects but lower than the major aspects. The open, expressive symbol of this aspect is also very different from those of the other aspects – its energy radiating vibrantly outwards rather than being enclosed.

The sextile is a very helpful aspect which possesses more versatility and avenues of expression than the far-reaching energy of the trine. Individuals who possess many sextiles in their charts are usually balanced, lively and interesting. The fact that sextile voids are similar in number to those of the major aspects and far less frequent than voids in the opposition suggests that this aspect is almost as influential as the conjunction or square, and certainly as potent as the trine. Voids in sextiles do therefore give a chart a somewhat barren appearance, although the placement of trines can help to mitigate this effect. None of my 400 sample charts possesses voids in both sextile and trine – a combination which could be extremely difficult for the subject.

Sextiles (and trines) represent earned karmic gifts. Voids in these aspects indicate that the subject has abused these gifts in a past lifetime and must therefore work much harder to achieve success in the present one.

Most people possess at least one sextile – namely the Pluto–Neptune sextile of the middle to late 1900s, which although generational and subtle in its effect, does help to supply some immunity from the barrenness of a complete sextile void.

CONJUNCTION VOIDS

These voids are not common, being applicable to approximately 4 per cent of the population. This is perhaps because Mercury and Venus often form conjunctions with the Sun, and with each other, and because the orb allowed for a conjunction is relatively wide. Conjunction aspects are usually powerful and can either be difficult or harmonious, according to the planets involved. Three or more conjunctions in a birth chart will usually reduce the number of signs and houses occupied and thereby engender a more condensed or intense type of person. Voids in conjunctions tend to open up the birth chart – the ten planets being spread more evenly and wider apart. Splash type shapings are far more common when there is a lack of conjunctions.

When a planet does not form a conjunction it stands alone – its energy not uniting with any other energy. A conjunction of two planets, such as Saturn and Mars, forms an energy which is representative of neither of the two planets when operating singly. Such an energy is often very powerful and unique, but it can also be difficult to manage, thereby becoming destructive and unhelpful. This is often the case when an outer planet conjuncts a personal planet. A conjunction works powerfully against other planets which form difficult aspects against it, but the challenge thrown out by the single planet stands little chance against the combined energy of the planets in conjunction. But when a chart is void in conjunctions each planet has to fight its own battles – the energy generated being weaker but more even.

People who possess a void in conjunctions are complex, but well-balanced, versatile individuals, usually lacking in dynamism but often spiritually aware, espcially if there are other powerful voids – such as unaspected planets – within the chart.

The ratio between famous and non-famous personalities who possess this void is in perfect proportion (from my sample of 400 charts) thus indicating that conjunction voids are neither conducive nor detrimental to fame or infamy.

OPPOSITION VOIDS

These tend to occur very evenly throughout the broad spectrum of the population. Opposition aspects cause imbalance of character, with a perpetual striving on behalf of the subject to find the correct balance. The slightest upsurge (or diminution) of energy from one of the planets involved in the aspect causes the extremely precarious balance to rise (or fall) and one of the planets to take command for a brief spell. After a while, however, the deposed planet begins to fight back and quickly rises. At the point of balance the scales are swiftly turned in favour of the rising planet, thereby engendering a change of energy. This extreme manifestation of elevation and subjugation is akin to a basic rhythmic energy which incites continuous changes of mood and direction within the subject's psyche. Those who possess opposition voids do not usually experience this see-saw shift of energy but a person who has the mutable signs (Gemini, Virgo, Sagittarius and Pisces) prominently placed in his birth chart may undergo similar patterns of expression.

A chart which is high in oppositions may encourage schizophrenia or dual personality syndromes, whereas voids in this aspect give the subject more potential for balance in self-expression, although a surfeit of challenging squares or quincunxes may lessen the beneficial effect of such a void.

Opposition voids occur in all types of chart shapings, but they are inevitable within Bundle shapings (as is the quincunx), and very common in Bowl and Bucket shapings, these three being more intense, confined and restricted in self-expression than the other shapings. A person with many oppositions, therefore, is more sensitive and open to external stimuli – sometimes too much so, and is easily swayed by pressure. They tend to rely more upon other people, and need approval and recognition in their lives. Generally speaking the opposition is a weak aspect, which only manifests in severe problems when the subject is reacting in a highly negative manner. Judging by the high number of opposition voids amongst the general population, the karmic lessons involved with this aspect are easily learned, but perhaps easily forgotten too. Generally speaking, this is a beneficial void which adds peace and balance to the individual's character.

TRINE VOIDS

A chart that is void in trines usually belongs to a person who seems to experience more than life's fair share of problems and traumas, but this apparent unfairness of distribution is, as always, an inheritance of a disturbed karma. Trine aspects represent karmically inherited gifts and talents which a subject is entrusted to use wisely during any given lifetime. A lack of trines (or sextiles) indicates an abuse of these gifts during a past existence. Abuse of this aspect can just as easily mean under-use as over-use. An ignored, or passive trine is a waste of a very special talent which has been given to us by God in order to help our spiritual advancement through life, and once neglected, needs to be restored to its former position through subsequent lives of karmic atonement, represented by more challenging aspects. Trines and sextiles are bestowed upon us as honours and should be used in daily life with confidence, discrimination and humility, not abused by an inflatory ego and greed, or wasted through neglect.

People who lack trines and/or sextiles can appear to be hard, unyielding, or depressive individuals – especially if the chart contains many squares and quincunxes, but their determination and desire to overcome adversity is also very strong, and eventually the extra effort which they expend can herald its rewards.

SQUARE VOIDS

After much study of the general effect of aspects, and aspect voids, I have come to the conclusion that the combative energy produced by two (or more) planets when in square to one another is the most difficult to control and utilize positively. An abundance of squares in a birth chart which contains only one or two trines or sextiles renders it difficult for the beneficial energy of these aspects to gain a hold, thereby enabling the energy of the squares to take complete control. The reverse situation, however – one or two squares in a chart which contains several trines and sextiles – appears to represent balance and ease. In this instance the squares are less obtrusive and easier to use in a harmonious way.

Many very famous, successful personalities possess very few squares in their charts. No squares at all, although uncommon, is extremely desirable, providing the chart is not littered with an abundance of other aspects. Usually, however, a chart without squares is generally low in aspects. An excellent example of this pattern is contained in the chart of Cliff Richard. A lack of squares, closely followed by a lack of conjunctions, is the highest karmic honour, and usually only occurs in the charts of old and learned souls. The combative, highly tense and extremely powerful energy of the square is missing. These people are more able to relax and enter into situations which they enjoy. There is usually something very pleasant or likeable about their general demeanour but they may be mistaken for weak personalities if their charts possess too many trines or sextiles. Several of the subjects in my sample who possess this void are extremely well-liked and naturally charming, but tend to lack ethics. Once again, this is really a situation in which the remaining aspects are taking control and the trines or sextiles being abused. Generally speaking a lack of squares produces an inner strength with an ability to forgive and blend well with all types of people. These individuals are also less likely to become aggressive or violent, although a powerful Mars or Pluto in an opposition aspect may mitigate the generally beneficial effect.

5

Minor Voids

The theory and practice of utilizing voids can be extended into several minor areas of astrological interpretation. When doing so, most birth charts contain at least one void other than those accounted for by the occurrence of unoccupied houses.

All birth charts are interesting but those which contain much additional data or a lack of data tend to be particularly interesting to the astrologer. The study of minor voids, although slightly less conclusive than that of the major voids, is none the less extremely worthwhile and highly absorbing.

LACK OF ANGULAR PLANETS

When does a planet cease to be angular? When it is 6, 8 or perhaps even 10 degrees away from one of the four angles or the Midheaven? Astrologers vary in opinion, but each must form his or her own rules and adhere to them. In my opinion a planet situated within an orb of 8 degrees on either side of one of the four angles or the Midheaven (8th, 9th, 10th or 11th house as applicable to the Equal House system of division) constitutes an angular planet. Planets situated in the third, sixth, ninth or twelfth houses are usually less conspicuous than when placed in the angular houses (fourth, seventh, tenth or first), but study from various sources, including my own, has proved that they are just as effective. It is, however, extremely tempting to regard a planet posited in an angular house which is within a 9–10 degree orb of the cusp as being angular. But even though these planets may seem to be strongly represented in the character of the subject, a line has to be drawn somewhere. Angular planets are usually given much credence in interpretation. They tend to shine forth like a beacon and can completely dominate the character of the individual who possesses such strongly placed planets. They often indicate particular strengths (or weaknesses). A chart without an angular planet, however, can appear to be strangely quiet or lacking in character. There is no immediate quality to home in upon (unless there is a stellium in a certain sign) and no instant planetary domination. Such charts can, therefore, appear to be less interesting. In essence, however, a person with no angular planets is often a very well-balanced individual, whose life is not ruled by one or two planets (unless one particular planet forms an excess of difficult aspects), but is able to react to life from the point of view of all the planets, because they are operating on a similar level. Individuals without angular planets often possess quiet, complex natures which underly an inner strength of character.

A lack of angular planets does not seem to detract from general talents and abilities or the capacity to become well-known, but it can produce a more 'all round' talent. Forty-three subjects from the sample 400 charts lacked angular planets. On a percentage ratio these were evenly distributed between the Famous and Non-famous categories, with 11 Famous and 32 Non-famous. The examples from the Famous category included such names as the Princess of Wales, Charles Dickens, Paul McCartney, Elizabeth Taylor and the composer Tchaikovsky. Another notable example from outside of the survey is Barbra Streisand.

I have always wondered if there was a specific astrological factor which drove a subject towards fame or notoriety, and in the past I had considered that tenth

BARBRA STREISAND

(Born on 24.4.1942 at 4.16 a.m. in New York, USA)

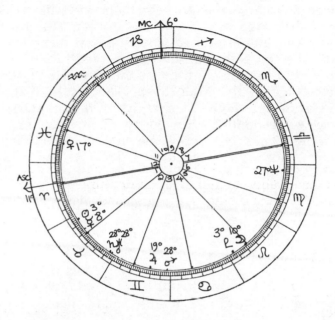

VOID DATA
Number of unoccupied houses – 5
Number of aspects – 14.   No semi-sextiles, quincunxes
or oppositions
Venus only square Jupiter.

No cardinal
No angular planets

CHART 6.   *Barbra Streisand*

house planets or angular planets played an important role in this energy. It would appear, however, that the very famous subjects mentioned above certainly did not need an angular planet to help them towards success. This result incited me to take the study a little further, and I became interested in discovering how many famous personalities possessed an unoccupied tenth house combined with a lack of ninth house angular planets or any planets conjunct the Midheaven. The resulting figures were surprisingly high. Twenty-five of the one hundred samples corresponded with the above criteria. Included within this 25 per cent were some more household names – Prince Andrew, Prince Edward, Fred Astaire, Charlie Chaplin, Sigmund Freud, Edward Kennedy, Louis Pasteur, Cliff Richard, Ringo Starr, Shirley Temple and many others. So although the tenth house and/or the Midheaven are regarded as driving forces behind the career, they do not necessarily need to be activated by planets to be prominent in a subject's life. In the long run, subjects without angular planets or planets in the tenth seem to be no less successful than people who possess strong tenth house placements and/or many angular planets.

On a karmic level it would appear that an angular planet signifies a quality within the individual that requires special attention during the present lifetime. A lack of angular planets indicates that the karmic lessons are evenly balanced between the planets and are therefore less powerful and restrictive in their effect.

DECANATE VOIDS

The study of decanates has not been allocated much attention by most astrologers, but the difference in characteristics between the three groupings of decanates within any one sign can provide much additional information about a person. Karmically, the decanates can be divided as follows:

BODY	MIND	SPIRIT
(Physical)	(Mental)	(Spiritual)
Degrees 0–9	Degrees 10–19	Degrees 20–29

Most individuals possess at least one planet in all three divisions, but usually one sector is prominent. Subjects whose charts contain a majority of Body degrees are usually more physical, materialistic, sensible and down to earth in their approach to life, but they also tend to lack spiritual insight. Individuals who possess a prominence of the Mind degrees are intelligent, intellectual, logical and communicative, but they can lack practical application if the Body degrees are low in comparison. The Spirit degrees are those which operate on a highly intuitive and spiritual level. A predominance of planets in these degrees usually inclines the subject towards a more enlightened mode of existence, but too little Body or Mind degrees can generate impracticality and/or over-sensitivity. Ideally there should be a balance between all three groups.

Complete voids in one of these decanates are not very common. Only twenty-three subjects from the 400 sample possessed a decanate void – eleven in the Body decanate, six in the Mind decanate and six in the Spirit decanate. In the Famous category only four of the 100 individuals possessed such a void – all of them occurring in the Physical degrees.

On a karmic level a lack of physical degrees seems to indicate stamina or inner strength rather than any weakness related to the 'Body' characteristics. Chris Evert Lloyd (renowned ladies tennis champion) is a good example of this overriding strength and determination, as are Sir Laurence Olivier and the pioneer of birth control Marie Stopes. A void in these degrees would seem to suggest a high level of karmic development, in which there is an innate talent or ability to use one's physical and practical prowess if needed. Amongst my seven Non-famous examples, however, it did seem to suggest a slight instability of character or a highly strung temperament. One such example is a chart belonging to a girl who suffers from severe epilepsy. A prominence of mental degrees in her chart endeavours to compensate for the lack of physically placed planets.

Unlike the Body voids, a lack of Mental or Spiritual degrees does not necessarily imply a high level of karmic development. A void in either one of these decanates can give rise to a surfeit of physical degrees, thereby imbuing the subject with an inclination to wallow in the physical expression of life. A void in the Mind degrees, however, can indicate a situation whereby the physical and spiritual degrees are evenly distributed, thus causing a split personality. The subject is torn between his or her materialistic and esoteric values.

From my sample charts, it would appear that a void in Mind degrees does not detract from the general intelligence, but the subject may appear to be less communicative or intellectual than they really are.

A lack of spiritual degrees does not usually represent a highly developed person unless there are several other important voids to consider. These individuals can be highly intelligent and practical, but without that essence of spiritual enlightenment their lives could be considered colourless or empty. It is very rare for a highly successful person to be totally lacking in spiritual degrees, for there is usually a magnetic or highly appealing aura surrounding a person whose chart is prominent in these degrees. It is interesting to note in this context that the UK Prime Minister John Major has this void in his chart.

The last degree in each decanate is important as it represents the highest, and therefore the most powerful for good or ill, within its category. Any person with more than one planet placed at any of these three highlighted degrees is likely to have the qualities of the relative decanate strongly emphasized. Nine is the highest physical degree – it can produce tremendous energy, vitality and strength, but also greed, over-acquisitiveness and vanity. Nineteen, the highest in the Mental category, usually gives a superb, retentive and analytical mind. These people are great thinkers, often bordering upon genius, but they must beware of the fine dividing line between sanity and insanity. Twenty-nine is the highest spiritual degree and many mediums, astrologers, healers or highly spiritual individuals have this degree prominent in their chart. It is such a powerful degree, however, that it is sometimes difficult for the individual to control the energy and it is a sad fact that a large number of people who lead traumatic lives or fall by the wayside via such escapist means as addiction, suicide, crime or violence, also tend to have at least one planet, or the Ascendant or Midheaven placed at this degree.

THE VOID OF COURSE MOON

This is a phenomenon which most astrologers recognize, but few use in the interpretation of natal charts. Every so often (not on a regular basis) the Moon is in a position whereby it will make no further *applying* major aspects (conjunction, square, trine, opposition or sextile) before leaving the sign it occupies. Immediately the Moon reaches zero degrees of a sign it can no longer be void. The easiest way to check whether a Moon is void is to look at the number of degrees it occupies. If placed within the first fifteen degrees of a sign it is extremely rare for it to be void. Occasionally it may be void when posited at 16–19 degrees – my eldest son has a void Moon placed at 19 degrees of Libra – but these early placements are very uncommon. Usually the degrees of occupation are somewhere within the third decanate (20–29 degrees) of a sign – and the closer the Moon is to 29 degrees the more likely it is to be void.

Quincunxes, semi-sextiles, or any other minor aspects are not considered strong enough to deter a void Moon – for instance, a planet placed at 28 degrees of Scorpio in quincunx aspect to the Moon at 27 degrees of Aries does not alleviate the phenomenon – the Moon is still regarded as being void.

Unaspected Moons need not necessarily be void. A Moon placed in early degrees of a sign – say 7 degrees of Aquarius – with no immediate aspects would still be regarded as possessing an applying square to a planet situated at 21 degrees of Taurus. The key to recognition is to look at the degrees of the Moon and make sure that it will not form any one of the five major aspects before it leaves the sign in which it is posited.

When the Moon moves into a void phase – a period which ranges from a few minutes up to approximately twenty-eight hours – time often seems to stand still. No new projects or highly active operations should be undertaken, no contracts signed and no new possessions should be acquired. Otherwise they may become null, void or unsuitable – according to the few astrologers who have written about the subject. They say it is time for reflection, peace and rejuvenation, a time when batteries (energy) should be recharged in order that the subject is ready for action when the Moon moves into a new sign. A few years ago I studied these theories from a personal viewpoint, and found them to be somewhat suspect – sometimes appearing to work and at other times failing to have any effect.

A high proportion of the population are born with a void Moon in their birth charts. From a survey of 250 charts which I studied in the early 1980s I deduced that around one in twelve people are born with this place-ment. But the figures from my 400 sample reveal a slightly higher percentage with an exceptionally high 1 in 8 ratio occurring within the 100 famous examples. The contribution of void Moons rendered by the immediate members of the royal family is also particularly high: Princess Margaret, Princess Diana, Prince Henry and Princess Eugenie all possess this placement. Other exam-ples of famous void Moon individuals are Elizabeth Taylor, Judy Garland, Margaret Thatcher and King Edward VII.

As with a lack of angular planets, Void of Course Moons do not seem to detract from the inherent potential towards fame or infamy, but most subjects born with this type of Moon do appear to suffer to some extent from the turmoils of their emotions. It is said that Void of Course Moon individuals do not react on a normal emotional level – they can be seemingly devoid of emotions or submerged in emotional drudgery. Many void Moon subjects learn to hide their emotions from an

JUDY GARLAND

(Born on 10.6.22 at 6.00 a.m. in Minnesota, USA)

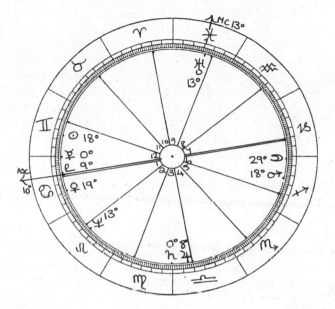

VOID DATA
Number of unoccupied houses – 6
Number of aspects – 15. No sextiles
No earth
Moon Void of Course

CHART 7. *Judy Garland*

early age. They do not fit easily into family life – always feeling different and misunderstood. These people suffer in silence whilst putting on a brave face simply because they do not know how to cope with their emotions. In a natal chart most void Moons have formed aspects from which they are separating – again indicating the pulling away of the emotions towards an empty space. Many void Moon people feel quite empty inside and immensely lonely, but there is always a reason for everything that happens within our lives, and it would seem that these people have probably abused their emotional gifts in a past life, and therefore have much to learn concerning emotional reactions in their future lives. Their present existence, however, seems to indicate stagnation, stillness or waiting. There is an inability to move forward, but perhaps it is this very barrier that is the fundamental basis of the lesson they are required to overcome.

Despite its name, the Void of Course Moon, unless unaspected, is not a true void, and because only true voids represent ease, inherent talent and learned lessons, this position of the Moon must be regarded as another challenge or karmic lesson in life.

LACK OF MAJOR PLANETARY CONFIGURATIONS

All planetary configurations require aspects. The more aspects there are in a chart the more cluttered, disorganized and contradictory are the characteristics of the individual. Only the grand trine is considered to be helpful whilst the T-square, grand cross and to a lesser extent the yod, are considered to be problematical. Certainly these challenging configurations can be worked upon and used positively, but very often the trauma and hardship involved within the karmic learning process is too overwhelming and the individual succumbs to an easier, more negative solution.

It is not an advantage to possess a T-square or a grand cross – both of which involve two major difficult aspects. Most individuals are more able to cope with life's problems when configurations such as these are not around. The yod, too, is not an easy configuration – its power and talent being accompanied by a nervous (but often unconscious) tension which must be overcome before the combination can be used positively. Even the favourable grand trine can inspire laziness and a casual acceptance of the inherent talents and abilities which it bestows.

All aspects relay messages concerning emphasis upon certain karmic lessons, and the major planetary configurations are further powerful extensions of these sometimes extremely fateful lessons. Even the grand trine bears a message which says, 'You have been given a remarkable talent – use it!'

Many people possess charts without one of the four major configurations. With regard to the T-square, grand cross and yod this may be a blessing rather than a lack, but if the subject works hard and learns much during his present lifetime he may be rewarded with the presence of a grand trine during his next lifetime.

Index